**OPPOSING
VIEWPOINTS®
SERIES**

WITHDRAWN

Development,
Land Use, and
Environmental Impact

Other Books of Related Interest

Opposing Viewpoints Series

Corporate Farming

Pesticides and GMOs

The Politics of Water Scarcity

At Issue Series

Environmental Racism and Classism

Green Cities

Pipelines and Politics

Current Controversies Series

Are There Two Americas?

Fracking

States' Rights and the Role of the Federal Government

> "Congress shall make no law … abridging the freedom of speech, or of the press."

First Amendment to the US Constitution

The basic foundation of our democracy is the First Amendment guarantee of freedom of expression. The Opposing Viewpoints series is dedicated to the concept of this basic freedom and the idea that it is more important to practice it than to enshrine it.

**OPPOSING
VIEWPOINTS®
SERIES**

Development,
Land Use, and
Environmental Impact

Srijita C. Pal, Book Editor

GREENHAVEN
PUBLISHING

Published in 2020 by Greenhaven Publishing, LLC
353 3rd Avenue, Suite 255, New York, NY 10010

Articles in Greenhaven Publishing anthologies are often edited for length to meet page
requirements. In addition, original titles of these works are changed to clearly present
the main thesis and to explicitly indicate the author's opinion. Every effort is made to
ensure that Greenhaven Publishing accurately reflects the original intent of the authors.
Every effort has been made to trace the owners of the copyrighted material.

Cover image: Robyn Beck/AFP/Getty Images

Cataloging-in-Publication Data

Names: Pal, Srijita C., editor.
Title: Development, land use, and environmental impact / edited by Srijita C. Pal.
Description: New York : Greenhaven Publishing, 2020. | Series: Opposing viewpoints
| Includes bibliographical references and index. | Audience: Grades 9-12.
Identifiers: ISBN 9781534505100 (library bound) | ISBN 9781534505117 (pbk.)
Subjects: LCSH: Land use--Juvenile literature. | Land use--Environmental
aspects--Juvenile literature. | Civil engineering--Juvenile literature.
Classification: LCC HD111.D484 2020 | DDC 333.73/13--dc23

Manufactured in the United States of America

Website: http://greenhavenpublishing.com

Contents

Chapter 3: Is Environmental Impact an Inevitable Side Effect of Land Use and Development?

Chapter 4: Why Is It Important to Consider the Effects of Land Development and Use on the Environment?

The Importance of Opposing Viewpoints

Perhaps every generation experiences a period in time in which the populace seems especially polarized, starkly divided on the important issues of the day and gravitating toward the far ends of the political spectrum and away from a consensus-facilitating middle ground. The world that today's students are growing up in and that they will soon enter into as active and engaged citizens is deeply fragmented in just this way. Issues relating to terrorism, immigration, women's rights, minority rights, race relations, health care, taxation, wealth and poverty, the environment, policing, military intervention, the proper role of government—in some ways, perennial issues that are freshly and uniquely urgent and vital with each new generation—are currently roiling the world.

If we are to foster a knowledgeable, responsible, active, and engaged citizenry among today's youth, we must provide them with the intellectual, interpretive, and critical-thinking tools and experience necessary to make sense of the world around them and of the all-important debates and arguments that inform it. After all, the outcome of these debates will in large measure determine the future course, prospects, and outcomes of the world and its peoples, particularly its youth. If they are to become successful members of society and productive and informed citizens, students need to learn how to evaluate the strengths and weaknesses of someone else's arguments, how to sift fact from opinion and fallacy, and how to test the relative merits and validity of their own opinions against the known facts and the best possible available information. The landmark series Opposing Viewpoints has been providing students with just such critical-thinking skills and exposure to the debates surrounding society's most urgent contemporary issues for many years, and it continues to serve this essential role with undiminished commitment, care, and rigor.

The key to the series's success in achieving its goal of sharpening students' critical-thinking and analytic skills resides in its title—

Opposing Viewpoints. In every intriguing, compelling, and engaging volume of this series, readers are presented with the widest possible spectrum of distinct viewpoints, expert opinions, and informed argumentation and commentary, supplied by some of today's leading academics, thinkers, analysts, politicians, policy makers, economists, activists, change agents, and advocates. Every opinion and argument anthologized here is presented objectively and accorded respect. There is no editorializing in any introductory text or in the arrangement and order of the pieces. No piece is included as a "straw man," an easy ideological target for cheap point scoring. As wide and inclusive a range of viewpoints as possible is offered, with no privileging of one particular political ideology or cultural perspective over another. It is left to each individual reader to evaluate the relative merits of each argument—as he or she sees it, and with the use of ever-growing critical-thinking skills—and grapple with his or her own assumptions, beliefs, and perspectives to determine how convincing or successful any given argument is and how the reader's own stance on the issue may be modified or altered in response to it.

This process is facilitated and supported by volume, chapter, and selection introductions that provide readers with the essential context they need to begin engaging with the spotlighted issues, with the debates surrounding them, and with their own perhaps shifting or nascent opinions on them. In addition, guided reading and discussion questions encourage readers to determine the authors' point of view and purpose, interrogate and analyze the various arguments and their rhetoric and structure, evaluate the arguments' strengths and weaknesses, test their claims against available facts and evidence, judge the validity of the reasoning, and bring into clearer, sharper focus the reader's own beliefs and conclusions and how they may differ from or align with those in the collection or those of their classmates.

Research has shown that reading comprehension skills improve dramatically when students are provided with compelling, intriguing, and relevant "discussable" texts. The subject matter of these collections could not be more compelling, intriguing, or urgently relevant to today's students and the world they are poised to inherit. The anthologized articles and the reading and discussion questions that are included with them also provide the basis for stimulating, lively, and passionate classroom debates. Students who are compelled to anticipate objections to their own argument and identify the flaws in those of an opponent read more carefully, think more critically, and steep themselves in relevant context, facts, and information more thoroughly. In short, using discussable text of the kind provided by every single volume in the Opposing Viewpoints series encourages close reading, facilitates reading comprehension, fosters research, strengthens critical thinking, and greatly enlivens and energizes classroom discussion and participation. The entire learning process is deepened, extended, and strengthened.

For all of these reasons, Opposing Viewpoints continues to be exactly the right resource at exactly the right time—when we most need to provide readers with the critical-thinking tools and skills that will not only serve them well in school but also in their careers and their daily lives as decision-making family members, community members, and citizens. This series encourages respectful engagement with and analysis of opposing viewpoints and fosters a resulting increase in the strength and rigor of one's own opinions and stances. As such, it helps make readers "future ready," and that readiness will pay rich dividends for the readers themselves, for the citizenry, for our society, and for the world at large.

Introduction

> *"The global food system has fundamentally altered our planet and the resource base humanity depends on. Food production is responsible for about a quarter of all greenhouse gas emissions and therefore a major driver of climate change. Agriculture occupies more than a third of the Earth's land surface and has led to reductions in forest cover and loss of biodiversity. Farming also uses more than two-thirds of all freshwater resources, and the over-application of fertilizers in some regions has led to dead zones in oceans."*
>
> —Marco Springmann,
> Oxford Martin Programme
> on the Future of Food[1]

Evidence suggests that humans began altering the environment in ways to suit themselves twelve thousand years ago during the Neolithic Revolution. The very first kind of these alterations came in the form of land use for agriculture. From very early on, the value of land has been clear.

Arguably the very first form of economic relationships was based on the lord, who owned the land, and the serf, who was bound to the land. Over the years, land use and planning resulted in never-before-seen stability of food sources. This agricultural revolution in turn led to the formation of the very first complex societies.

Beginning in the 1760s, the Industrial Revolution sparked many changes, including the acceleration of land development. As a result, land became valuable not only for what it could produce naturally but also for what modes of production could occur on it.

Finally, with the movement of humans into cities, the level of development as well as the level of land use skyrocketed. In 1700, a mere 5 percent of the world's land was in use by humans. By 2000, this number jumped to 55 percent.[2]

Land has not only become a source of wealth but also a valuable natural resource. From extracting minerals from the earth to diverting the flow of rivers to suit human agricultural practices, the very building blocks of modern societies are based on altering the environment in ways to make the planet a more habitable and productive place. Thanks to deforestation over centuries, the planet looks very different than it once did. A greater percentage of earth's land is in use by humans than ever before. In fact, about half of the world's surface area has been converted into land for grazing animals or cultivating crops.[3] The impact on the environment is noticeable on the geological scale as well—many of the previously fertile areas of the world have turned into deserts because of extensive human activity in the region, and the destruction of forests continues at an unprecedented rate to make room for development and to supply the raw materials for other industries.

In the 1800s, a lack of governmental oversight of privately owned lands caused poor management of traffic, overcrowding, and inadequate waste disposal. The latter also contributed to the spread of diseases. Uncontrolled urbanization and its effects led to municipalities being given the power to regulate private land use to protect public health and safety.[4] The latest concern for land development is urban sprawl. This, in part, has been addressed by new legal methods. In the United States, zoning laws have been adopted by most state legislatures to make sure land use follows a set of guidelines. Additionally, federal laws have been put into place to protect the natural environment and mitigate pollution of the environment in many areas of the world.

The debate over land use continues as the world population has risen and human activity has rapidly escalated. While some see development as the pinnacle of human achievement and the use of the surrounding environment as an innate aspect of civilization, others see development, especially on a mass scale, as intrusive to the surrounding environment and a detriment to the future survival of the species. With fears about climate change at the forefront, ethical considerations arise about land use.

In chapters titled "How Do Different Kinds of Land Use Affect the Environment Differently?," "Does the Negative Impact of Development on the Environment Outweigh Its Benefits?," "Is Environmental Impact an Inevitable Side Effect of Land Use and Development?," and "Why Is It Important to Consider the Effects of Land Development and Use on the Environment?," the viewpoint authors who have contributed to *Opposing Viewpoints: Development, Land Use, and Environmental Impact* debate the many facets of this complex topic and suggest solutions for a better future.

Notes

1. Quoted in Aristos Georgiou, "Devastating Climate Change Coming? Here's How We Can Feed 10 Billion People Sustainably by 2050," *Newsweek*, October 10, 2018.

2. E. C. Ellis, K. Klein Goldewijk, S. Siebert, D. Lightman, and N. Ramankutty, "Anthropogenic Transformation of the Biomes, 1700 to 2000," *Global Ecology and Biogeography* 19 (2010): 589–606.

3. P. Kareiva, S. Watts, R. McDonald, and T. Boucher, "Domesticated Nature: Shaping Landscapes and Ecosystems for Human Welfare," *Science* 316, no. 5833 (2007): 1866–69.

4. John N. Nolon, "Historical Overview of the American Land Use System A Diagnostic Approach to Evaluating Governmental Land Use Control," *Pace Environmental Law Review* 23, no. 3 (September 2006): 821–53. https://law.pace.edu/files/landuse/Land_Use_System.pdf.

OPPOSING
VIEWPOINTS®
SERIES

CHAPTER 1

How Do Different Kinds of Land Use Affect the Environment Differently?

Chapter Preface

L and is an important part of our planet. Along with labor and capital, land is one of the three major factors of production. That means every nation's economy is greatly impacted by land and how it is used—and abused. During the early years of planet Earth, much of its land was covered with forestation. Now, forested areas have decreased by an astonishing rate.

The way a society uses land also affects the environment. Agriculture booms that resulted from the need to feed a growing population also resulted in water pollution and wildlife extinction.

Major population shifts in the past few decades have contributed to the growth of cities around the world. Urban residents consume alarming amounts of energy, so much so that they can even change entire environments that surround them.

Land use is a critical factor to a society's well-being. Changes in land use can be negative, but they can also promote economic development and social progress. It is important that governments engage in land use planning to balance the protection of natural lands with increases in property values and quality of life. However, there are critics who believe government errs on the side of overregulation.

There is no question that land use and changes to land use affect the environment, in both big and small ways. But the types of development and ways of developing can have different impacts. The viewpoints in this chapter explore this topic in varied and interesting ways.

"*Land use regulation must strike a
balance between private property
rights and the public interest.*"

Land Use Changes Have Economic, Social, and Environmental Impacts

JunJie Wu

*In the following viewpoint, JunJie Wu argues that changes to land
use have affected the United States in the past quarter century. Land
is one of a nation's three major factors of economic production,
and changes to its use can have far-reaching economic, social, and
environmental impacts. The author contends that proper conservation
efforts and smart regulation can ensure that land use change drives
economic development and social progress. Wu is the Emery N. Castle
Professor of Resource and Rural Economics in the Department of
Agricultural and Resource Economics at Oregon State University.*

As you read, consider the following questions:

1. By how much did the total area of US developed land increase during the past twenty-five years, according to the viewpoint?
2. What did Oregon's Measure 37 provide?
3. Besides water pollution, what can urban runoff cause, according to the viewpoint?

Major land-use changes have occurred in the United States during the past 25 years. The total area of cropland, pastureland and rangeland decreased by 76 million acres in the lower 48 states from 1982 to 2003, while the total area of developed land increased by 36 million acres or 48%. What are the potential economic, social, and environmental impacts of land use changes? How does land use change affect agriculture and rural communities? What are the important economic and environmental implications for commodity production and trade, water and soil conservation, open space preservation, and other policy issues? This article addresses some of these issues and their policy implications.

Socioeconomic Impacts

Land is one of three major factors of production in classical economics (along with labor and capital) and an essential input for housing and food production. Thus, land use is the backbone of agricultural economies and it provides substantial economic and social benefits. Land use change is necessary and essential for economic development and social progress.

Land use change, however, does not come without costs (see Table 1). Conversion of farmland and forests to urban development reduces the amount of lands available for food and timber production. Soil erosion, salinization, desertification, and other soil degradations associated with intensive agriculture

---

Table 1. Socioeconomic Impacts of Land-Use Changes

- Conversion of farmland and forests to urban development reduces the amount of land available for food and timber production
- Soil erosion, salinization, desertification, and other soil degradations associated with agricultural production and deforestation reduce land quality and agricultural productivity
- Conversions of farmland and forests to urban development reduce the amount of open space and environmental amenities for local residents
- Urban development reduces the "critical mass" of farmland necessary for the economic survival of local agricultural economies
- Urban development patterns not only affect the lives of individuals, but also the ways in which society is organized
- Urban development has encroached upon some rural communities to such an extent that the community's identify has been lost
- Suburbanization intensifies income segregation and economic disparities among communities
- Excessive land use control, however, may hinder the function of market forces
- Land use regulations that aim at curbing land development will raise housing prices, making housing less affordable to middle- and low-income households
- Land use regulation must strike a balance between private property rights and the public interest

---

and deforestation reduce the quality of land resources and future agricultural productivity (Lubowski et al. 2006).

Urbanization presents many challenges for farmers on the urban fringe. Conflicts with nonfarm neighbors and vandalism, such as destruction of crops and damage to farm equipment, are major concerns of farmers at the urban fringe (Lisansky, 1986). Neighboring farmers often cooperate in production activities, including equipment sharing, land renting, custom work, and irrigation system development. These benefits will disappear when neighboring farms are converted to development. Farmers may no longer be able to benefit from information sharing and formal and informal business relationships among neighboring farms. Urbanization may also cause the "impermanence syndrome" (i.e., a lack of confidence in the stability and long-run profitability of farming), leading to a reduction in investment in new technology or machinery, or idling of farmland (Lopez, Adelaja, and Andrews, 1988).

As urbanization intensifies, agricultural and nonagricultural land use conflicts become more severe. This may lead to an increase in local ordinances designed to force farmers to pay for some of the negative impacts generated by agriculture. As the nearest input suppliers close because of insufficient demand for farm inputs, a farmer may have to pay more for inputs or spend more time to obtain equipment repairs (Lynch and Carpenter, 2003). Competition for labor from nonagricultural sectors may raise farmers' labor costs. When the total amount of farmland falls below a critical mass, the local agricultural economy may collapse as all agricultural supporting sectors disappear.

Urbanization also presents important opportunities to farmers. The emergence of a new customer base provides farmers new opportunities for selling higher value crops. For example, Lopez, Adelaja, and Andrews (1988) found that vegetable producers tend to receive higher prices in urbanized areas. The explosion of nurseries, vegetable farms, vineyards, and other high-value crop industries in many suburban areas illustrates how quickly agricultural economies can evolve. Many farmers have shown remarkable adaptability in adjusting their enterprises to take advantage of new economic opportunities at the urban fringe. They farm more intensively in areas with high population density (Lockeretz 1988). More than half the value of total US farm production is derived from counties facing urbanization pressure (Larson, Findeis, and Smith 2001).

Urbanization has changed rural communities in many places. In some rural areas, urban sprawl has encroached to such an extent that the community itself has been lost. In other areas, the lack of opportunities has turned once-viable communities into ghost towns. Urban sprawl intensifies income segregation and economic disparities between urban and suburban communities (Wu, 2006). Cities tend to gain lower-income residents and lose upper-income population. Between 1969 and 1998, the share of low-income families in central cities grew from 21.9% to 25.5% compared with a decline from 18.3% to 16.6% for high-income households (US Department of Housing and Urban Development 2000). The change in income mix led to a smaller tax base and the need for more social services in urban communities.

Suburbanization brings urban and rural people and problems together. Most land areas are rural, most watersheds are in rural places, and most of the atmosphere exists above rural space. Urbanites and agencies have legitimate concerns about the use and condition of rural natural resources, just as rural populations have legitimate concerns about urban-based pressures on the natural world. These shared interests in the natural environment have important economic, social, and political implications, which may profoundly impact society in the future.

In response to the increasing urbanization, many local governments have imposed strict land use control. Some of the efforts have been quite successful in slowing down development. For example, Wu and Cho (2007) found that local land use regulations reduced land development by 10% in the five western states between 1982 and 1997, with the largest percent reduction occurring in Washington (13.0%), followed by Oregon (12.6%), California (9.5%), Idaho (4.7%), and Nevada (2.8%). A potential consequence of land use regulation is higher housing prices, which make housing less affordable to middle- and low-income households. There is sufficient evidence to support the linkage between land use regulation and housing affordability. Two recent Harvard University studies found that land use regulation reduces housing affordability in the Greater Boston Area (Glaeser and Ward 2006; Glaeser and Gyourko 2002). Cho, Wu and Boggess (2003)

LAND USE CHANGE AND ENVIRONMENTAL SUSTAINABILITY

United Nations (UN) world population data indicates that it took about 150 years (1750–1900) for the world's population to more than triple from 0.7 to about 2.5 billion, whereas it only took 40 years (1950–1990) for the population to double again to 5 billion. It is estimated that more than 1 billion people were added to the world's population between 1995 and 2008. The unprecedented growth in the human population in the last centuries translates to escalated resource consumption, as manifested in relatively high rates of agriculture and food production, industrial development, energy production and urbanization. These human enterprises lead to local land-use and land-cover changes that, when aggregated, have a global-scale impact on climate, hydrology, biogeochemistry, biodiversity and the ability of biological systems to support human needs.

Sustainability is the guiding principle for international environmental policy and decision-making in the twenty-first century. It cuts across several international agenda, including the UN Framework Convention on Climate Change, the United Nations Convention to Combat Desertification, and the Convention on Biological Diversity, among others. The sustainability principle obscures the distinction between

analyzed the causes and consequences of land use regulations across counties in five western states and found that land use regulation increased average housing prices between 1.3 and 4.7%, depending on the intensity of land use regulations in a county.

Land use control must strike a balance between private property rights and the public interest. Oregon ballot measures 37 and 49 highlight the difficulty and controversy of the balancing act. In an attempt to protect private property rights from regulatory taking, Oregon voters passed Measure 37 in 2004. Measure 37 provides that the government must compensate the owner of private real property when a land use regulation reduces its "fair market value." In lieu of compensation, the government may choose to "remove, modify or environment and development and encourages the fusion of global change research and sustainable development. There is a growing international community of researchers working on themes that are central to understanding land-use and land-cover change as a major driver of environmental change at local, regional and global scales. … The Global Land Project, jointly established by the International Human Dimensions Program on Global Environmental Change and the International Geosphere Biosphere Program is the foremost international global change project promoting LCS for environmental sustainability. The GLP is planned around three research foci seeking to integrate a range of research questions towards an improved understanding of the dynamics of land change, the causes and consequences of land change, and assessment of system outcomes, notably vulnerability and resilience of land systems. These GLP-related efforts focus on sustainability issues arising from changes and responses to the synergistic operations of societal and environmental subsystems of land. They provide an opportunity for international scholars with different disciplinary backgrounds to address these complex issues arising from human-environment interactions that cannot be satisfactorily dealt with by core disciplinary methods alone.

"Land-Use Change and Environmental Sustainability," by Ademola K. Braimoh and M. Osaki, Springer Nature, November 8, 2017.

not apply" the regulation. Measure 37 was ruled unconstitutional by a lower court, but was upheld by the Oregon State Supreme Court. By October 19, 2007, 6,814 claims had been filed, requesting almost $20 billion in compensation (Oregon Department of Land Conservation and Development 2007). In an effort to reverse or modify Measure 37, Oregon voters approved Measure 49 on Nov. 6, 2007 to "ensure that Oregon law provides just compensation for unfair burdens while retaining Oregon's protection for farm and forest land uses and the state's water resources" (ODLCD, 2008). Measure 49 essentially modifies Measure 37 by replacing "waivers" of regulations with authorizations to establish a limited number of home sites.

In sum, land use change provides many economic and social benefits, but comes at a substantial economic cost to society. Land conservation is a critical element in achieving long-term economic growth and sustainable development. Land use policy, however, must strike a balance between private property rights and the public interest.

Environmental Impacts

Land-use change is arguably the most pervasive socioeconomic force driving changes and degradation of ecosystems. Deforestation, urban development, agriculture, and other human activities have substantially altered the Earth's landscape. Such disturbance of the land affects important ecosystem processes and services, which can have wide-ranging and long-term consequences (Table 2).

Table 2. Environmental Impacts of Land-Use Changes

- Land use and land management practices have a major impact on natural resources including water, soil, air, nutrients, plants, and animals
- Runoff from agriculture is a leading source of water pollution both in inland and coastal waters
- Draining wetlands for crop production and irrigation water diversions has had a negative impact on many wildlife species
- Irrigated agriculture has changed the water cycle and caused groundwater levels to decline in many parts of the world
- Intensive farming and deforestation may cause soil erosion, salinization, desertification, and other soil degradations
- Deforestation adds to the greenhouse effect, destroys habitats that support biodiversity, affects the hydrological cycle and increases soil erosion, runoff, flooding and landslides.
- Urban development causes air pollution, water pollution, and urban runoff and flooding
- Habitat destruction, fragmentation, and alteration associated with urban development are a leading cause of biodiversity decline and species extinctions
- Urban development and intensive agriculture in coastal areas and further inland is a major threat to the health, productivity, and biodiversity of the marine environment throughout the world

---

Farmland provides open space and valuable habitat for many wildlife species. However, intensive agriculture has potentially severe ecosystem consequences. For example, it has long been recognized that agricultural land use and practices can cause water pollution and the effect is influenced by government policies. Runoff from agricultural lands is a leading source of water pollution both in inland and coastal waters. Conversions of wetlands to crop production and irrigation water diversions have brought many wildlife species to the verge of extinction.

Forests provide many ecosystem services. They support biodiversity, providing critical habitat for wildlife, remove carbon dioxide from the atmosphere, intercept precipitation, slow down surface runoff, and reduce soil erosion and flooding. These important ecosystem services will be reduced or destroyed when forests are converted to agriculture or urban development. For example, deforestation, along with urban sprawl, agriculture, and other human activities, has substantially altered and fragmented the Earth's vegetative cover. Such disturbance can change the global atmospheric concentration of carbon dioxide, the principal heat-trapping gas, as well as affect local, regional, and global climate by changing the energy balance on Earth's surface (Marland et al. 2003).

Urban development has been linked to many environmental problems, including air pollution, water pollution, and loss of wildlife habitat. Urban runoff often contains nutrients, sediment and toxic contaminants, and can cause not only water pollution but also large variation in stream flow and temperatures.

Habitat destruction, fragmentation, and alteration associated with urban development have been identified as the leading causes of biodiversity decline and species extinctions (Czech, Krausman and Devers 2000; Soulé 1991). Urban development and intensive agriculture in coastal areas and further inland are a major threat to the health, productivity, and biodiversity of the marine environment throughout the world.

Policy Implications

Land use provides many economic and social benefits, but often comes at a substantial cost to the environment. Although most economic costs are figured into land use decisions, most environmental externalities are not. These environmental "externalities" cause a divergence between private and social costs for some land uses, leading to an inefficient land allocation. For example, developers may not bear all the environmental and infrastructural costs generated by their projects. Farmland produces both agricultural commodities and open space. Although farmers are paid for the commodities they produce, they may not be compensated for the open space they provide. Plus, market prices of farmlands may be below their social values.

Such "market failures" provide a justification for private conservation efforts and public land use planning and regulation. Private trusts and non profit organizations play an important role in land conservation. For example, the American Farmland Trust claims that it has helped to protect more than one million acres of America's best farm and ranch land. The Nature Conservancy has protected more than 117 million acres of ecologically important lands. However, some have questioned whether private conservation efforts crowd out or complement public efforts for land conservation.

Land use regulation can take many different forms. The traditional command and control approach often involves zoning, density regulation, and other direct land use controls. Although these policies can be quite effective as regulatory tools, they could lead to substantial social welfare loss in the form of higher housing prices, smaller houses, and inefficient land use patterns (Cheshire and Sheppard 2002; Walsh 2007).

Incentive-based policies are increasingly used to influence private land use decisions. These policies may include development impact fees, purchases of development rights (PDRs), preferential property taxation, and direct conservation payments. From 1998 to 2006, voters approved 1,197 conservation initiatives in local and state referenda in the United States, providing a total $34 billion for land and open space preservation (Trust for Public Land 2007). The implementation of locally based, long-term conservation plans has been touted as a critical element in achieving "smart growth" (US Environmental Protection Agency 2007).

The incentive-based approach has many advantages over direct land use control. For example, a development impact fee can be used to achieve both the optimal pace and pattern of land development, a shortcoming of zoning regulations (Wu and Irwin, 2008). However, zoning may be preferred from a practical viewpoint as well as in cases where the environmental costs of land conversion are highly uncertain. In situations where the natural and human systems interact in complex ways, thresholds and nonlinear dynamics are likely to exist, and the environmental costs could be very high and sensitive to additional development. In such cases, zoning may be preferred. The policy challenge, however, is to know when the system is in the neighborhood of such thresholds.

While federal spending on land-related conservation programs has increased substantially over the last twenty five years, the federal government has yet to articulate a clear vision of how land use should be managed (Daniels, 1999). Most land use controls are in the hands of local governments in the United States, and the level of control varies considerably across counties and municipalities. Some local governments have few land use controls, while others are actively involved in land use planning and regulation.

Land use regulation is a contentious issue in many communities, particularly those facing rapid urbanization. Proponents argue that land use planning protects farmland, forests, water quality, open space, and wildlife habitat and, at the same time, increases property value and human health. Conversely, uncontrolled development will destroy the natural environment and long-term economic growth. Critics of land use regulation call those fears overblown. They argue that urban development is an orderly market process that allocates land from agriculture to urban use, and that governments tend to over regulate because they rarely bear the costs of regulation. The stakes are high in this debate. Any policy measures that aim at curbing urban development will ultimately affect a key element of the American way of life, that is, the ability to consume a large amount of living space at affordable prices. Policymakers must resist the temptation to attribute all "irregular" land use patterns to market failures and impose stringent land use regulations that may hinder the function of market forces. They should try to identify the sources of market failures that cause "excessive development" and address problems at their roots. Land use regulation must strike a balance between private property rights and the public interest.

> *"In recent decades, increasing concern for the environment and sustainability has compelled many governments to continuously adjust their land-use policies to balance multiple uses of land resources."*

Interactions Between Society and the Environment Require Aggressive Responses

Radoslava Kanianska

In the following excerpted viewpoint, Radoslava Kanianska argues that human influences on the land have increased, due to rapid population growth and ever greater food requirements. The author analyzes the influence of agriculture on land use, environment, and ecosystem services, taking into account the driving forces, pressures, states, impacts, and response. Kanianska is on the Faculty of Natural Sciences at Matej Bel University in Banská Bystrica, Slovakia.

As you read, consider the following questions:

1. What percentage of the planet's land is covered with agricultural ecosystems, according to the viewpoint?
2. Why have earth's forests decreased so dramatically over time, according to the author?
3. What is eutrophication, as explained in the viewpoint?

With the growing world population the requirements are grown to cover the food demand. Human expansion throughout the world caused that agriculture is a dominant form of land management globally, and agricultural ecosystems cover nearly 40% of the terrestrial surface of the Earth. Agricultural ecosystems are interlinked with rural areas where more than 3 billion people live, almost half of the world's population. Roughly 2.5 billion of these rural people derive their livelihoods from agriculture. Thus, population and land-use trends are considered to be the main driving forces for agriculture. Besides these driving forces, EEA[7] further distinguished the so-called external and internal driving forces originating from market trends, technological and social changes, as well as the policy framework.

For many economies, especially those of developing countries, agriculture can be an important engine—driving force—of economic growth. Approximately three-quarters of the world's agricultural value added is generated in developing countries where agriculture constitutes the backbone of the economy. But not only in the developing countries but also in the developed countries agriculture has always been the precursor to the rise of industry and services.[8]

Population Trend

In the twentieth century, the world population grew four times.[9] Although demographic growth rates have been slowing since the late 1970s, the world's population has doubled since then, to approximately 7 billion people currently and is projected to increase to over 9 billion by 2050. But already millions people are still suffering from hunger and malnutrition. The latest available estimates indicate that about 795 million people in the world (just over one in nine) were undernourished in 2014–2016. Since 1990–1992, the number of undernourished people has declined by 216 million globally, a reduction of 21.4%. The vast majority of the hungry people live in the developing regions. The overall hunger reduction trends in the developing countries since 1990–1992 are connected with changes in large populous countries (China, India).[10] Paradoxically, most of people suffering from hunger and malnutrition are in rural areas and only 20% are in city slums. According to FAO, 50% of them are small peasants, 20% are landless, 10% are nomadic herdsmen or small fishermen, and 20% live in city slums. In the developing countries, this rural social class is, above all, often a victim of marginalization and exclusion from its governing classes (political, economic, and financial) as well as from the urban milieu where there is a concentration of power and knowledge, and therefore money, including funds for development. Often the urban and rural worlds are separated. Whereas in the EU the farming population constitutes only 5% of the total population, it is about 50% in China, 60% in India, and between 60 and 80% in sub-Saharan Africa.[11]

In past, Slovakia was typical agrarian country. Even during the nineteenth century the vast majority of the population worked in agriculture, but with the beginning of the twentieth century the decreasing trend began and continued to the present. In 1921, 60.4% of the working population was engaged in agriculture, after 1945, it was 48.1%. In 2012, 50,400 people worked in agriculture[12] which represented 2.2% of the working population, and 2.76 workers worked per 100 ha of agricultural land which was less than EU-27 average (8.81 workers per 100 ha of agricultural land).[13]

Land Use

The global land area is 13.2 billion ha. Of this, 12% (1.6 billion ha) is currently in use for cultivation of agricultural crops, 28%

(3.7 billion ha) is under forest, and 35% (4.6 billion ha) comprises grasslands and woodland ecosystems. The world's cultivated area has grown by 12% over the past 50 years. Globally, about 0.23 ha of land is cultivated per head of the world's population.[14] In 1960, it was 0.5 ha of cropland per capita worldwide. In Europe, about one- half of land is farmed and arable land is the most common form of agricultural land. Twenty- five percent of Europe's land is covered by arable land and permanent crops, 17% by pastures and mixed mosaics, and 35% by forests. The average amount of cropland and pasture land per capita in 1970 was 0.4 and 0.8 ha and by 2010 this had decreased to 0.2 and 0.5 ha per capita, respectively.[15]

Such a state is a result of dynamic land-use and land-cover changes. Humans have altered land cover for centuries, but recent rates of change are higher than ever.[16]

Land-use change reflected in land-cover change and land-cover change is a main component of global environmental change,[17] affecting climate, biodiversity, and ecosystem services, which in turn affect land-use decision. Land-use change is always caused by multiple interacting factors. The mix of driving forces of land-use change varies in time and space. Highly variable ecosystem conditions driven by climatic variations amplify the pressure arising from high demands on land resources. Economic factors define a range of variables that have a direct impact on the decision making by land managers. Technology can affect labor market and operational processes on land. Demographic factors, such as increase and decrease of population, and migration patterns have a large impact on land use. Life-cycle features arise and affect rural as well as urban environments. They shape the trajectory of land-use change, which itself affects the household's economic status.

The development of the present ecosystems in the postglacial period (Holocene) depended on significant changes in climate. Warming in the postglacial period, about 10,000 years ago, created conditions of back migration of individuals species from their refuges, where they were protected during the glacial periods. After the neolithic revolution, human society began to influence more noticeably the development of natural ecosystems. About half of the ice-free land surface has been converted or substantially modified by human activities. Forest covered about 50% of the Earth's land area 8000 years ago, as opposed to 30% today. Agriculture has expanded into forests, savannas, and steppes in all parts of the world to meet the demand for food and fiber.

The central and north Europe were almost completely naturally covered by forests. Only high mountain and alpine rocky localities were without forest cover. Nowadays Europe is a mosaic of landscapes, reflecting the evolutionary pattern of changes that land use has undergone in the past. The greatest concentration of farmland is found in Eastern Europe, where also Slovakia lies, with more than half of its land area in crop cover.[18] Europe is one of the most intensively used continents on the globe. Despite the long tradition of human impact investigation on the environment and vegetation in Europe, there are few comparable studies in North America. This difference is often attributed to the shorter duration of intensive human impact in most of North America versus Europe. As a result, prior studies in the United States have generally been restricted to local investigations.[19]

During the past three centuries, in many developing countries and countries with transition economies, growing demand for food due to an increasing population has caused substantial expansion of cropland, accompanied by shrinking primary forests and grassland areas.[20] Based on many studies, in China between 1700 and 1950, cropland area increased and forest coverage decreased. Similarly in India, between 1880 and 2010, cropland area has increased (from 92 to 140.1 million ha), and forest land decreased (from 89 to 63 million ha).[21] But in the past 50 years, over world rapid urbanization has been evident.[22] Migration in its various forms is the most important demographic factor causing land-use change at timescales of a couple of decades.[23] Rapid economic growth is accompanied by a shift of land from agriculture to industry, infrastructure, road network, and residential use. Countries in

East Asia, North America, and Europe have all lost cultivated land during their periods of economic development.[18] The dramatic growth and globalization of China's economy and market since economy reforms in 1978 have brought about a massive loss of croplands, most of which were converted to urban areas and transportation routes during 1978–1995.[24]

In Slovakia land-use trends are in many aspects similar to EU development. In 2013, of the total area of Slovakia agricultural land covered 48.9% (2,397,041 ha) and forest land 41.1% (2,017,105 ha). The highest share of used agricultural land was represented by arable land (58.9%) followed by permanent grasslands (36.1%). The average amount of agricultural land per capita was 0.44 ha.[25] Cereals are the main growing crops. Since 1990, decrease in agricultural land was recorded, often in favor of built-up area. Analysis of historical land-use changes at Liptovská Teplička cadastre showed that the landscape has undergone changes in land-use and cover during the 224 years. From the long-term point of view, gradual afforestation and permanent grassland conversion to forest land was observed where forest land increased from 67.7% in 1782 to 83.7% in 2006.[26]

Pressure

Agriculture in the last century has evolved from self-sufficiency to surplus in some parts of the world. Thus, transformation was connected with intensification and specialization of production as main trends in European or North American agriculture accompanied by negative impact on the environment. Agricultural intensification is defined as higher levels of inputs and increased output of cultivated or reared products per unit area and time.[27] Over the past 50 years, agricultural production has grown between 2.5 and 3 times, thanks to significant increase in the yield of major crops.[14] Changing land-use practices have enabled world grain harvests to double from 1.2 to 2.5 billion tonnes per year between 1970 and 2010. Globally, since 1970, there has been a 1.4-fold increase in the numbers of cattle and buffalo, sheep and goats, and increases of 1.6- and 3.7-fold for pigs and poultry, respectively.[28]

The mix of cropland expansion and agricultural intensification has varied geographically. Tropical Asia increased its food production mainly by increasing fertilizer use and irrigation. Most of Africa and Latin America increased their food production through both agricultural intensification and extensification. In western Africa cropland expansion was accompanied by a decrease in fertilizer use and a slight increase in irrigation.[18] Agriculture is the single largest user of freshwater resources, using a global average of 70% of all surface water supplies.

Intensification and Specialization of Agriculture

Intensification and specialization have been predominant trends in EU countries including Slovakia for several decades. Between 1965 and 2000 there was a 6.87-fold increase in nitrogen fertilization, a 3.48-fold increase in phosphorous fertilization while irrigated land area expanded 1.68 times, contributing to a 10% net increase in land in cultivation.[29] Strong intensification in Europe in contrast to other countries is obvious if we compare selected indicators, e.g., fertilizer consumption or livestock density. In Slovakia, the maximum intensification level was reached during the socialistic era in 80th. However, since 1990, there are signs of a trend toward a more efficient use of agricultural inputs as a result of not very favorable economic situation of farms but also as a consequence of different environmental measures implementation. During 1980–2010 in Slovakia, indicators concerning to agricultural intensification dropped, in case of fertilizer consumption by 73%, the pesticides consumption by 77%. This period is typical in livestock number reduction, in case of cattle by 71, pigs 73, and sheep 37%.

Intensification is connected with increasing release of atmospheric emissions through management of land and livestock, and thus agriculture release to the atmosphere significant amounts of greenhouse gases emissions of CO_2, CH_4, and N_2O[33] and ammonia emissions. The agricultural sector is currently responsible for the vast majority of ammonia emissions in the European Union. Agriculture contributes to about 47 and 58% of total anthropogenic emissions of CH_4 and N_2O, respectively. Annual GHG emissions from agricultural production in 2000–2010 were estimated at 5.0–5.8 GtCO$_2$ CO$_2$ eq/year while annual GHG flux from land use and land-use change activities accounted for approximately 4.3–5.5 GtCO$_2$eq/year. The enteric fermentation and agricultural soils represent together about 70% of total emissions, followed by paddy rice cultivation (9–11%), biomass burning (6–12%), and manure management (7–8%).[34] Annual GHG emissions from agriculture are expected to increase in coming decades due to escalating demands for food and shift in diet. However improved management practices and emerging technologies may permit a reduction in emissions per unit of food produced. In Slovakia, due to decrease number of livestock also decreasing trend in GHG and ammonia emissions were observed since 1990.

State

Intensive management practices in agriculture escalating rates of land degradation threatens most crop and pasture land throughout the world. Worldwide, more than 12 million hectares of productive arable land are severely degraded and abandoned annually. Increased pressure is connected with deterioration of the state of environment, mainly soil and water.

Soil

Soil is the most fundamental asset on farms. Its quality that directly affects provisioning ecosystem services is strongly affected by management practices. The state of soils can be assessed by the help of indicators on soil contamination, erosion, and compaction.

Soil contamination implies that the concentration of a substance in soil is higher than would naturally occur. Agricultural activities contribute to soil contamination by introducing pollutants or toxic substances such as cadmium by application of mineral phosphate fertilizers or organic pollutants by pesticide application. Comprehensive inventories and databases on local and diffuse soil contamination are lacking on the global or regional extent. Estimates show that about 15% of land in the EU-27 exhibits a surplus in excess of 40 kg N/ha.[37] In Slovakia, data from the soil monitoring showed that only 0.4% of the total soil cover is contaminated by heavy metals.[38]

The loss of soil from land surfaces by soil erosion has been significantly increased by human activities. Each year about 10 million ha of cropland are lost due to soil erosion.[39] In Slovakia, 32% of agricultural land is threatened by water and 5% by wind erosion, respectively.[36]

Since the 1950s, pressure on agricultural land has increased considerably also owing to agricultural modernization and mechanization what caused next serious environmental problem— soil compaction. Overuse of machinery, intensive cropping, short crop rotations, intensive grazing, and inappropriate soil management leads to compaction.[40] Soil compaction problems, in various degrees, are found in virtually all cropping systems throughout the world. They are of particular significance where intensive mechanization has been adopted on soils subject to high rainfall or irrigation.[41] According to estimation approximately 600,000 ha of agricultural land is compacted in Slovakia.[42]

The effect of farming on soil causing soil compaction expressed as soil penetrometric resistance (PR measured to 20 cm depth in MPa) was investigated in May 2014 at Liptovská Teplička cadastre, on soil type Rendzina with four different land-use (AL, arable land; M, meadow; AG, abandoned grasslands; FL, forest land). The different land use and practices reflected in different PR values. The highest mean PR value was measured in AL (1.52 MPa), followed by M and FL (same value of 1.08 MPa), and abandoned grasslands (0.90 MPa).[43] Measured values show at compaction in arable land. But there is necessary to take into account possibility that PR value in AL could be also the lowest among observed different land-use sites. Such situation can be observed when the measurement is done immediately after some technological operation, e.g., ploughing, contributing to turning the soil over, and diminishing higher soil horizons compaction.

Water

Agriculture is both cause and victim of water pollution. Evidence for elevated nitrate and phosphate contents on farm, in drains, streams and rivers, and lakes is partial and tends to be specific to a given location and circumstance. Global phosphorus flux to the ocean increased 3-fold to about 22 Tg per year by the end of the twentieth century.

Nitrate is the most common chemical contaminant in the world's aquifers. An estimate for continental USA in the 1990s indicates that returns to water are close to 20% of total applied agricultural nitrogen, with up to 25% lost in gaseous form. Mean nitrate levels have increased by about 36% in global waterways since 1990.[44]

Pesticides contaminate surface water and groundwater. They can reach surface water through runoff from treated plants and soil. Contamination of water by pesticides is widespread, and groundwater pollution due to pesticides is a worldwide problem.[45]

Impact

Impacts are commonly the result of multiple stressors. Agriculture exerts pressure on the environment that is both beneficial and harmful and can result in both positive and negative environmental impacts. The wide variation in farming systems and practices throughout the world, and differing environmental characteristics mean that the effects of agriculture on the environment arise at site-specific level but can have impacts at local to global level.

Traditional Landscape Disappearance

The disappearance of traditional agricultural landscape is an ongoing process, accompanying the general trend of agricultural abandonment in Europe.[46] In Slovakia, traditional agricultural landscape is described as agricultural ecosystems that consist of mosaics of small-scale arable fields or permanent agricultural cultivations such as grasslands, vineyards, and high-trunk orchards or early abandoned plots with a low succession degree.[47] Important parts of such landscape are linear landscape elements (hedges, tree lines, stone walls).

In Slovakia, traditional extensive farming with individual farmer attitude to landscape was transformed to collectivization with overall interest in land exploitation.[48] Collectivization caused small-scale parcels managed by individual farmers to be consolidated into large blocks (polygons) managed by large co-operative farms and resulted in a decrease of the mosaic of arable land and grasslands. At Liptovská Teplička cadastre during 1956–1990, number of polygons decreased from 15 to 2 at arable land, and from 82 to 29 at permanent grasslands.[26] In addition, the management of traditional agricultural landscapes structures decreased rapidly after collectivization. Nowadays the main barriers in ideal management are unfavorable subsidies in agriculture and the financial inaccessibility of modern tools and machinery together with inadequate market and the weak support of local government.[49]

Contribution to Climate Change

Anthropogenic land-use activities and changes in land use/cover caused changes superimposed on the natural fluxes. Land-cover changes are responsible for surface and vegetation modifications what reflects in surface albedo and thus surface-atmosphere energy exchanges, which have an impact on regional climate. Terrestrial ecosystems are important sources and sinks of carbon and thus land-use changes reflect also in the carbon cycle. The important contribution of local evapotranspiration to the water cycle—that is precipitation recycling— as a function of land cover highlighted yet another considerable impact of land-use/cover change on climate, at a local to regional scale.[50]

The influence of land use/cover on soil temperature was investigated at Liptovská Teplička cadastre study site in May

2014 where 10 measurements in depth of 5 and 25 cm at four different land-use plots (AL, arable land; M, meadow; AG, abandoned grasslands; FL, forest land) were done by insert soil thermometer. The highest mean soil temperature was recorded in AL in 5 cm depth (4.6°C), the lowest in FL in 5 cm depth (3.5°C). Measured values show how plant cover and its microclimate functions are important and can affect soil temperature.

Agriculture is unique among economic sectors releasing GHG emissions and thus contributing to climate change. Agricultural activities lead, in fact, not only to sources but also to important sinks of CO_2. Agricultural contribution to greenhouse gases accounts for 13.5% of global greenhouse gas emissions.[51] At the same time, agricultural production is fully climate and several further natural conditions dependent. Every change in climate has not only short-term but also long-term consequences. Climate change brings an increase in risk and unpredictability for farmers— from warming and related aridity, from shifts in rainfall patterns, and from the growing incidence of extreme weather events.

On the other hand, agriculture can also positively contribute to climate change mitigation. The utilization of agricultural residues as raw materials in a biorefinery is a promising alternative to fossil resources for production of energy carriers and chemicals, thus mitigating climate change and enhancing energy security.[52]

Biodiversity Losses

Land use, specifically in agriculture, has great impact on biodiversity. Another aspect contributing to biodiversity decline is that humans today depend for survival on tiny fraction of wild species that has been domesticated. Yet only 14 of 148 species weighing 45 kg or more were actually domesticated. Similarly, worldwide there are about 200,000 wild species of higher plants, of which only about 100 yielded valuable domesticates.[53]

All long-term historical land-use changes responsible for natural ecosystems conversion to seminatural ecosystems or artificial systems contributed to the extensive changes in biodiversity composition and ecological processes. Agriculture plays an important role in these processes and is responsible for biodiversity decline. Over the past 50 years, ecosystems have changed more rapidly than at any other period of human history.[62] This period is connected with high agricultural intensification in many parts of the world. Land-use changes have been shown to be one of the leading causes of biodiversity loss in terrestrial ecosystems.[54, 55] To demonstrate the impact of land use and land management on soil biota quantitative analysis of earthworm was done at Liptovská Teplička cadastre in May 2014 when earthworms were hand sorted, weighted, and numbered from seven soil monoliths (35 cm × 35 cm × 20 cm) placed in line in 3 m distance in four different land-use plots (AL, arable land; M, meadow; AG, abandoned grasslands; FL, forest land). The earthworms may be used as bioindicator because they are very sensitive to both chemical and physical soil parameters. Earthworm biomass or abundance can offer a valuable tool to assess different environmental impacts such as tillage operations, soil pollution, different agricultural input, trampling, and industrial plant pollution.[56] The highest mean number (87.5 individuals m^{-2}) and earthworm body biomass (40.3 g m^{-2}) was recorded in M, the lowest in AG (5.8 individuals m^{-2} and 5.9 g m^{-2} body biomass).[49] Relatively high number and earthworm biomass in AL at Liptovská Teplička cadastre is consequence of organic farming.

Though intensified land use is undeniably the main cause of biodiversity loss. There is an increasing expectation that productive agricultural landscapes should be managed to preserve or enhance biodiversity.[57]

Eutrophication

Eutrophication is a process of pollution that occurs when a lake or stream becomes overrich in plant nutrients as a consequence it becomes overgrown in algae and other aquatic plants. The major impacts of eutrophication due to overloading with nitrogen and phosphorus nutrients are changes in the structure and functioning of marine ecosystems, reduced biodiversity, and reduced income from fishery, mariculture, and tourism. The main source of nitrogen run-off from agricultural land brought to the sea via rivers. Atmospheric deposition of nitrogen may also contribute significantly to the nitrogen load. This nitrogen originates partly from ammonia evaporation from animal husbandry. Most of the phosphorus comes from households and industries discharging treated or untreated wastewater to freshwater directly to the sea, and from soil erosion.

Human activity has increased N fluxes. In 1970s, an explosive increase in coastal eutrophication in many parts of the world correlates well with the increased production of reactive N for agriculture and industry.[45] Eutrophication is a global environmental problem. In EU, there is marked variation in groundwater nitrate concentration between different geographical regions with high concentration in Western Europe and very low concentrations in Northern Europe. The lack of a general decrease is due to continued high emissions from agriculture.[58]

Agroecosystem Services Degradation

Agroecosystems both provide and rely on ecosystem services to sustain production food, fiber, and other harvestable goods. Increases in food and fiber production have often been achieved at the cost of other critical services.

Services that help to support production of harvestable goods can be considered as services to agriculture. These services include soil structure and fertility enhancement, nutrient cycling, water provision, erosion control, pollination, and pest control, among others. Ecological processes that detract from agricultural production can be considered disservices to agriculture and include pest damage, competition for water, and competition for pollination. Management of agricultural ecosystems also affects flows of ecosystem services and disservices (or diminution of naturally occurring services) from production landscape to surrounding areas. Disservices from agriculture can include degradation or loss of habitat, soil, water quality, and other off-site, negative impacts.[59]

Provision of ecosystem services in farmlands is directly determined by their design and management[60] and strongly influenced by the function and diversity of the surrounding landscape.[61] The Millenium Ecosystem Assessment[62] reported that approximately 60% (15 out of 24) of services measured in the assessment were being degraded or unsustainably used as a consequence of agricultural management and other human activities.

Response

In recent decades, increasing concern for the environment and sustainability has compelled many governments to continuously adjust their land-use policies to balance multiple uses of land resources. These policies have caused changes in cropland and its spatial distribution. There are different environmental objectives incorporated into agrienvironment measures, training programs, support for investments in agricultural holdings, protection of the environment in connection with agriculture and landscape conservation, support to improving the processing and marketing of agricultural products. Organic farming or low-input farming systems are examples where support for the processing or marketing of their products can help in achieving environmental objectives. In 2013, there were 43.1 million hectares of organic agricultural land, including conversion areas. The regions with the largest areas of organic agricultural land are Oceania and Europe.[63] In Slovakia, organic farming area covered 8.4% of the total agricultural land.[36]

Conclusion

Agriculture is a dominant form of land management globally. Rapid population growth as primary driving force connected with increasing food requirements generate great pressure on future land use, environment, natural resources, and ecosystem services. The DPSIR framework approach helped us to analyze selected indicators having the cause-effect relationships between the economic, social, and environmental sectors.

Recent rates of land-use and cover changes are higher than ever. In many developing countries and countries with transition economies, growing demand for food has caused expansion of cropland. Extensive agricultural systems are slowly intensified. In developed countries, economic growth has been recently accompanied by a shift of land from agriculture to industry, road network, and residential use. Extensive forms of agriculture used in past mainly in Europe and North America were transformed into industrial-style agriculture accompanied by intensification and specialization. The large inputs of fertilizers, pesticides, fossil fuels have large, complex effects on the environment. Agriculture releases significant amounts of greenhouse gases and ammonia emission to the atmosphere. It is the single largest user of freshwater resources. Intensive management practices escalating rates of land degradation, soil and water deterioration. The effects on the environment arise at site-specific level but can have impact at local to global levels. Land-cover changes cause the disappearance of traditional agricultural landscape and are responsible for vegetation modifications which have an impact on regional climate, carbon sequestration, and biodiversity losses. Agriculture also has impact on the natural systems and ecosystem services on which humans depend.

Future challenges relating to greater pressure on environment, natural resources, and climate change imply that a "business as usual" model in agriculture is not a viable option. Green growth is a new method that places strong emphasis on the complementarities between the economic, social, and environmental dimensions of sustainable development. Thus, the main role of future agriculture is its transformation into good productive but a sustainable system that can be effective for centuries without adverse effect on natural resources on which agricultural productivity depends.

Notes

7. EEA. *Integration of environment into EU agriculture policy—the IRENA indicator- based assessment report*. Copenhagen: EEA; 2006. 64 p.

8. FAO. *FAO statistical yearbook 2013. World food and agriculture*. Rome: FAO; 2013. 307 p.

9. UNEP. *Towards a green economy: pathway to sustainable development and poverty reduction. A synthesis for policy makers*. Nairobi: UNEP; 2011. 52 p.

10. FAO, IFAD, WFP. *The state of food insecurity in the world 2015. Meeting the 2015 international hunger targets: taking stock of uneven progress*. Rome: FAO; 2015. 62 p.

11. Feyder J. Commentary I: agriculture: a unique sector in economic ecological and social terms. In: *Trade and environment review 2013. Wake up before it is too late. Make agriculture truly sustainable now for food security in a changing climate*. Geneva: UNCTAD; 2013. p. 9–12.

12. MARDSR. *Report on agriculture and food industry in the Slovak republic. Green report*. Bratislava: MARDSR; 2013. 68 p. (in Slovak).

13. Szabo L, Grznár M. Labour and performance of agriculture in the Slovak republic. *Economics of Agriculture*. 2015;XV/3:4–13 (in Slovak).

14. FAO. *The state of the world's land and water resources for food and agriculture (SOLAW)—managing systems at risk*. Rome: FAO and London: Earthscan; 2011. 308 p.

15. EEA. *The European environment—state and outlook 2010: synthesis*. Copenhagen: EEA; 2010. 212 p.

16. Hansen MC, Stehman SV, Potapov PV. Quantification of global gross forest cover loss. *Proceedings of the National Academy of Sciences of the United States America*. 2010;107:8650–8655.

17. Foley JA, DeFries RS, Asner GP, Barford C, Bonana G, Carpenter SR, Chapin FS, et al. Global consequences of land use. *Science*. 2005;80(309):570–574.

18. Ramankutty N, Foley JA, Olejniczak NJ. People on the land: changes in global population and croplands during the 20th Century. *AMBIO: A Journal of the Human Environment*. 2002;31:251–257.

19. Foster DR. Land-use history (1730–1990) and vegetation dynamics in central New England, USA. *Journal of Ecology*. 1992;80:753–772.

20. Liu M, Tian H. China's land cover and land use change from 1700 to 2005: estimations from high-resolution satellite data and historical archives. *Global Biogeochemical Cycles*. 2010;24:1–18.

21. Tian H, Banger K, Bo T, Dadhwal VK. History of land use in India during 1880–2010: large-scale land transformations reconstructed from satellite data and historical archives. *Global and Planetary Change*. 2014;121:78–88.

22. Miao L, Zhu F, He B, Ferrat M, Liu Q, Cao X, Cui X. Synthesis of China's land use in the past 300 years. *Global and Planetary Change*. 2013;100:224–233.

23. Geist HJ, Lambin EF. Proximate causes and underlying driving forces of tropical deforestation. *BioScience*. 2002;52(2):143–50.

24. Chen J. Rapid urbanization in China: a real challenge to soil protection and food security. *Catena*. 2007;69:1–15.

25. IGCCSR. *Statistical yearbook on land resources in the Slovak republic*. Bratislava: IGCCSR; 2015. 130 p. (in Slovak).

26. Kanianska R, Kizeková M, Nováček M, Zeman M. Land-use and land-cover changes in rural areas during different political systems: a case study of Slovakia from 1782 to 2006. *Land Use Policy.* 2014;36:554–566.

27. Matson PA, Parton WJ, Power AG, Swift MJ. Agricultural intensification and ecosystem properties. *Science.* 1997;277:504–509.

28. FAOSTAT. FAOSTAT database. Food and Agriculture Organisation of the United Nations; 2013. Available at: http://faostat.fao.org/.

29. Tilman D, Socolow R, Foley JA, Hill J, Larson E, Lyind L, Pacala S, Reilly J, Searchinger T, Somerville C, Williams R. Beneficial biofuels—the food, energy, and environment trilemma. *Science.* 2009;325:270–271.

33. Paustin K, Babcock BA, Hatfield J, Lal R, McCarl BA, McLaughhlin S, Mosier A. et al. Agricultural mitigation of greenhouse gases: science and policy options. CAST report; 2004. 18 p.

34. Smith PM, Bustamante H, Ahammad H, Clark H, Dong EA, Elsiddig H, Haberl R. et al. Agriculture, forestry and other land use (AFOLU). In: *Climate change 2014: mitigation of climate change.* Contribution of working group III to the fifth assessment report of the IPCC. Cambridge, UK and USA: Cambridge University Press; 2014. 112 p.

36. MESR, SEA. *State of the environment report of the Slovak republic 2014.* Bratislava, Banská Bystrica: SEA; 2015. 208 p.

37. JRC IES EC. The state of soil in Europe. A contribution of the JRC to the EEA's environment state and outlook report-SOER 2010. Ispra: JRC IES EC; 2012. 78 p.

38. Kobza J. Soil and plant pollution by potentially toxic elements in Slovakia. *Plant, Soil and Environment.* 2005;51:243–248.

39. Pimentel D, Burgess M. Soil erosion threatens food production. *Agriculture.* 2013;3:443–463.

40. Hamza MA, Anderson WK. Soil compaction in cropping systems. A review of the nature, causes and possible solutions. *Soil & Tillage Research.* 2004;82:121–145.

41. Soane BD, Ouwerker C. *Soil compaction in crop production. Developments in agricultural engineering 11.* Netherlands: Elsevier; 1994. 684 p.

42. Fulajtár E. Assessment and determination of the compacted soils in Slovakia. In: *Advanced in geoecology.* Catena Verlag; 2000. p. 384–387.

43. Kanianska R, Jadudová J. Evaluation of selected biotic and abiotic soil parameters having impact on ecosystem services. In: Kukla J, Kuklová M, editors. *Proceedings, Zvolen 11 June 2015.* Bratislava: SSPLPVV SAV, Zvolen: ÚEL SAV; 2015. p. 32–36.

44. WWDR4. Managing water along the livestock value chain. Chapter 18. *World water development report.* Rome: FAO; 2011.

45. Turral H, Mateo-Sagasta X, Burke J. *Water pollution from agriculture: a review.* Rome: FAO; 2012. 173 p.

46. Gerard F, Petit S, Smith G, Thomson A, Brown N, Manchester S, Wadsworth R. et al. Land cover change in Europe between 1950 and 2000 determined employing aerial photography. *Progress in Physical Geography.* 2010;34:183–205.

47. Dobrovodská M, Špulerová J, Štefunková D, Halabuk A. Research and maintenance of biodiversity in historical structures in the agricultural landscape of Slovakia. In: Barančoková M, Krajčí J, Kollár J, Belčáková I, editors. *Landscape Ecology—Methods, Applications and Interdisciplinary Approach.* Bratislava: ILE SAS; 2010. p. 131–140.

48. Bezák P, Petrovič F. Agriculture, landscape, biodiversity: scenarios and stakeholder perceptions in the Polonini national park (NE Slovakia). *Ecology.* 2006;25(1):82–93.

49. Lieskovský J, Bezák P, Špulerová J, Lieskovský T, Koleda P, Dobrovodská M, Bürgi M, Gimmi U. The abandonment of traditional agricultural landscape in Slovakia—analysis of extent and driving forces. *Journal of Rural Studies.* 2015;37:75–84.

50. Lambin EF, Geist HJ, Lepers E. Dynamics of land-use and land-cover change in tropical regions. *Annual Reviews of Environmental Resources.* 2003;28:205–241.

51. IPCC. *The fourth assessment report of the Intergovernmental Panel on climate change.* Geneva: IPCC; 2007. 112 p.

52. Cherubini F, Ulgiati S. Crop residues as raw materials for biorefinery systems—a LCA case study. *Applied Energy.* 2010;87:47–57.

53. Diamond J. Evolution, consequences and future of plant and animal domestication. *Nature.* 2002;418:700–707.

54. Daily GC, Polasky S, Goldstein J, Kareiva PM, Mooney HA, Pejchar L. et al. Ecosystem services in decision making: time to deliver. *Frontiers in Ecology and the Environment.* 2009;7(1):21–28.

55. Reidsma P, Telenburg T, van den Berg M, Alkemade R. Impacts of land-use change on biodiversity: an assessment of agricultural biodiversity in the European Union. *Agriculture, Ecosystems and Environment.* 2006;114(1):86–102.

56. Paoletti MG. The role of earthworms for assessment of sustainability and as bioindicators. *Agriculture, Ecosystems and Environment.* 1999;74:137–155.

57. Weeks ES, Mason N. Prioritising land-use decisions for the optimal delivery of ecosystem services and biodiversity protection in productive landscape. In: Grillo O, editor. *Biodiversity—the dynamic balance of the planet.* Rijeka, Croatia: InTech; 2014. p. 1–32.

58. EEA. Eutrophication in Europe's coastal waters. Topic report 7/2001. Copenhagen: EEA; 2001. 86 p.

59. Garbach K, Milder JC, Montenegro M, Karp DS, DeClerck FAJ. Biodiversity and ecosystem services in agroecosystem. In: Van Alfen N, editor. *Encyclopedia of Agriculture and Food Systems*, Volume 2. Netherlands: Elsevier; 2014. p. 21–40.

60. Zhang W, Ricketts T, Kremen C, Carney K, Swinton S. Ecosystem services and disservices to agriculture. *Ecological Economics.* 2007;64:253–260.

61. Kremen C, Ostfeld R. A call to ecologists: measuring, analysing, and managing ecosystem services. *Frontiers in Ecology and the Environment.* 2005;3:540–548.

62. MEA. *Millenium ecosystem assessment synthesis report.* USA, Washington D.C.: Island Press; 2005. 155 p.

63. Willer H, Lernoud J. The world of organic agriculture 2015: summary. In: RIOA FiBL& IFOAM: *the world of organic agriculture. Statistics and emerging trends; 2015.* p. 24–30.

> "*In only 200 years, the world's urban population has grown from 2 percent to nearly 50 percent of all people. The most striking examples of the urbanization of the world are the megacities of 10 million or more people.*"

Urbanization Is an Environmental Force to Be Reckoned With

Barbara Boyle Torrey

In the following viewpoint, Barbara Boyle Torrey argues that more than half the world's population is living in urban areas. The viewpoint was written in 2004, and since then urbanization has only increased. The author describes the differences in consumption patterns of urban dwellers as compared to their rural counterparts and contends that around the world those who live in cities use so much energy that they can alter entire environments, such as creating "heat islands" that can change local weather patterns. Torrey is a visiting scholar at the Population Reference Bureau. She has held several research positions, including chief of the Center for International Research at the US Census Bureau.

As you read, consider the following questions:

1. Are urban fertility rates higher or lower than rural fertility rates?
2. According to the viewpoint, what is the rate of cars per person in the United States?
3. In the absence of a strong government to combat urban environmental challenges, what can become important, according to the author?

Human beings have become an increasingly powerful environmental force over the last 10,000 years. With the advent of agriculture 8,000 years ago, we began to change the land.[1] And with the industrial revolution, we began to affect our atmosphere. The recent increase in the world's population has magnified the effects of our agricultural and economic activities. But the growth in world population has masked what may be an even more important human-environmental interaction: While the world's population is doubling, the world's urban population is tripling. Within the next few years, more than half the world's population will be living in urban areas.[2]

The level and growth of urbanization differ considerably by region. Among developing countries, Latin American countries have the highest proportion of their population living in urban areas. But East and South Asia are likely to have the fastest growth rates in the next 30 years. Almost all of future world population growth will be in towns and cities. Both the increase in and the redistribution of the earth's population are likely to affect the natural systems of the earth and the interactions between the urban environments and populations.

The best data on global urbanization trends come from the United Nations Population Division and the World Bank.[3] The UN, however, cautions users that the data are often imprecise because the definition of urban varies country by country. Past projections of urbanization have also often overestimated future rates of growth. Therefore, it is important to be careful in using urbanization data to draw definitive conclusions.

The Dynamics of Urbanization

In 1800 only about 2 percent of the world's population lived in urban areas. That was small wonder: Until a century ago, urban areas were some of the unhealthiest places for people to live. The increased density of populations in urban areas led to the rapid spread of infectious diseases. Consequently, death rates in urban areas historically were higher than in rural areas. The only way urban areas maintained their existence until recently was by the continual in-migration of rural people.[4]

In only 200 years, the world's urban population has grown from 2 percent to nearly 50 percent of all people. The most striking examples of the urbanization of the world are the megacities of 10 million or more people. In 1975 only four megacities existed; in 2000 there were 18. And by 2015 the UN estimates that there will be 22.[5] Much of the future growth, however, will not be in these huge agglomerations, but in the small to medium-size cities around the world.[6]

The growth in urban areas comes from both the increase in migration to the cities and the fertility of urban populations. Much of urban migration is driven by rural populations' desire for the advantages that urban areas offer. Urban advantages include greater opportunities to receive education, health care, and services such as entertainment. The urban poor have less opportunity for education than the urban nonpoor, but still they have more chance than rural populations.[7]

Urban fertility rates, though lower than rural fertility rates in every region of the world, contribute to the growth of urban areas. Within urban areas, women who migrated from rural areas have more children than those born in urban areas.[8] Of course, the rural migrants to urban areas are not a random selection of the rural population; they are more likely to have wanted fewer children even if they had stayed in the countryside. So the difference between the fertility of urban migrants and rural women probably exaggerates the impact of urban migration on fertility.

In sub-Saharan Africa, the urban fertility rates are about 1.5 children less than in rural areas; in Latin America the differences are almost two children.[9] Therefore, the urbanization of the world is likely to slow population growth. It is also likely to concentrate some environmental effects geographically.

Environmental Effects of Urbanization

Urban populations interact with their environment. Urban people change their environment through their consumption of food, energy, water, and land. And in turn, the polluted urban environment affects the health and quality of life of the urban population.

People who live in urban areas have very different consumption patterns than residents in rural areas.[10] For example, urban populations consume much more food, energy, and durable goods than rural populations. In China during the 1970s, the urban populations consumed more than twice as much pork as the rural populations who were raising the pigs.[11] With economic development, the difference in consumption declined as the rural populations ate better diets. But even a decade later, urban populations had 60 percent more pork in their diets than rural populations. The increasing consumption of meat is a sign of growing affluence in Beijing; in India where many urban residents are vegetarians, greater prosperity is seen in higher consumption of milk.

Urban populations not only consume more food, but they also consume more durable goods. In the early 1990s, Chinese households in urban areas were two times more likely to have a TV, eight times more likely to have a washing machine, and 25 times more likely to have a refrigerator than rural households.[12] This increased consumption is a function of urban labor markets, wages, and household structure.

Energy consumption for electricity, transportation, cooking, and heating is much higher in urban areas than in rural villages.

How Changes in Land Use Impact Waters

Land uses that impact water resources include agriculture, forestry, urbanization, recreation, and industrialization. Irrigation of lands changes the use and distribution of water. The removal of surface water and groundwater for irrigation changes the water's natural distribution and impacts the ecosystems that depend upon it. Demand for water to irrigate crops usually occurs when there is insufficient precipitation during the growing season, potentially causing stream and groundwater levels to be reduced. In addition, irrigation waters that return to either groundwater or surface waters can contain salts, pesticides, or have elevated levels of nutrients such as nitrate and phosphorous.

These contaminants in turn can cause harm to plant and animal life that depend on the returned water. If wetlands are drained, biological impacts may be substantial because wetlands are some of the most biologically productive ecosystems on Earth. Between 1780 and 1980, an estimated 60 million acres of wetlands in the Mississippi River Basin were drained.

The Everglades in south Florida are an excellent example of how land use changes, specifically changes in water flow, can impact wetlands. In 1948, Congress authorized the Central and Southern Florida Project for Flood Control and Other Purposes. Through

For example, urban populations have many more cars than rural populations per capita. Almost all of the cars in the world in the 1930s were in the United States. Today we have a car for every two people in the United States. If that became the norm, in 2050 there would be 5.3 billion cars in the world, all using energy.[13]

In China the per capita consumption of coal in towns and cities is over three times the consumption in rural areas.[14] Comparisons of changes in world energy consumption per capita and GNP show that the two are positively correlated but may not change at the same rate.[15] As countries move from using noncommercial forms of energy to commercial forms, the relative price of energy this act, levees were constructed to divert surface water to control flooding, and drainage ditches were dug to lower groundwater levels so agriculture and residential areas could be developed in marsh and swamp lands. Flood control efforts focused on directing interior waters through canals to coastal areas. The drainage ditches quickly lowered groundwater levels. Within a few decades these flood and drainage systems changes caused:

- Elimination of approximately 1,500,000 million acres of wetlands,
- Reduction in the number of species located in the Everglades; such as the Florida panther, snail kite, and the American crocodile,
- Depletion of the water supply needed by the human population, and the
- Increased likelihood of wildfires.

The removal of water from streams and groundwater systems to supply cities, and the land use changes associated with the development of the city, have consequences on the natural environment. For example, infiltration of water is reduced as the result of construction of highways, streets, parking lots and buildings. A reduction of infiltration can also increase runoff and the likelihood of flooding.

"How Do Changes in Land Use Impact Water Resources?" American Geosciences Institute.

increases. Economies, therefore, often become more efficient as they develop because of advances in technology and changes in consumption behavior. The urbanization of the world's populations, however, will increase aggregate energy use, despite efficiencies and new technologies. And the increased consumption of energy is likely to have deleterious environmental effects.

Urban consumption of energy helps create heat islands that can change local weather patterns and weather downwind from the heat islands. The heat island phenomenon is created because cities radiate heat back into the atmosphere at a rate 15 percent to 30 percent less than rural areas. The combination of the increased energy consumption and difference in albedo (radiation) means that cities are warmer than rural areas (0.6 to 1.3 C).[16] And these heat islands become traps for atmospheric pollutants. Cloudiness and fog occur with greater frequency. Precipitation is 5 percent to 10 percent higher in cities; thunderstorms and hailstorms are much more frequent, but snow days in cities are less common.

Urbanization also affects the broader regional environments. Regions downwind from large industrial complexes also see increases in the amount of precipitation, air pollution, and the number of days with thunderstorms.[17] Urban areas affect not only the weather patterns, but also the runoff patterns for water. Urban areas generally generate more rain, but they reduce the infiltration of water and lower the water tables. This means that runoff occurs more rapidly with greater peak flows. Flood volumes increase, as do floods and water pollution downstream.

Many of the effects of urban areas on the environment are not necessarily linear. Bigger urban areas do not always create more environmental problems. And small urban areas can cause large problems. Much of what determines the extent of the environmental impacts is how the urban populations behave—their consumption and living patterns—not just how large they are.

Health Effects of Environmental Degradation

The urban environment is an important factor in determining the quality of life in urban areas and the impact of the urban area on the broader environment. Some urban environmental problems include inadequate water and sanitation, lack of rubbish disposal, and industrial pollution.[18] Unfortunately, reducing the problems and ameliorating their effects on the urban population are expensive.

The health implications of these environmental problems include respiratory infections and other infectious and parasitic diseases. Capital costs for building improved environmental infrastructure—for example, investments in a cleaner public transportation system such as a subway—and for building more hospitals and clinics are higher in cities, where wages exceed those paid in rural areas. And urban land prices are much higher because of the competition for space. But not all urban areas have the same kinds of environmental conditions or health problems. Some research suggests that indicators of health problems, such as rates of infant mortality, are higher in cities that are growing rapidly than in those where growth is slower.[19]

Urban Environmental Policy Challenges

Since the 1950s, many cities in developed countries have met urban environmental challenges. Los Angeles has dramatically reduced air pollution. Many towns that grew up near rivers have succeeded in cleaning up the waters they befouled with industrial development. But cities at the beginning of their development generally have less wealth to devote to the mitigation of urban environmental impacts. And if the lack of resources is accompanied by inefficient government, a growing city may need many years for mitigation. Strong urban governance is critical to making progress. But it is often the resource in shortest supply.[20] Overlapping jurisdictions for water, air, roads, housing, and industrial development frustrate efficient governance of these vital environmental resources. The lack of good geographic information systems means that many public servants are operating with cataracts. The lack of good statistics means that many urban indicators that would inform careful environmental decisionmaking are missing.[21]

When strong urban governance is lacking, public-private partnerships can become more important.[22] These kinds of partnerships can help set priorities that are shared broadly, and therefore, implemented. Some of these public-private partnerships have advocated tackling the environmental threats to human health first. "Reducing soot, dust, lead, and microbial disease presents opportunities to achieve tangible progress at relatively low cost over relatively short periods," concluded conferees at a 1994 World Bank gathering on environmentally sustainable development.[23] But ultimately there are many other urban environmental priorities that produce chronic problems for both people and the environment over the long term that also have to be addressed.

Much of the research that needs to be done on the environmental impacts of urban areas has not been done because of a lack of data and funding. Most of the data that exist are at a national level. But national research is too coarse for the environmental improvement of urban areas. Therefore, data and research at the local level need to be developed to provide the local governments with the information they need to make decisions. Certainly the members of the next generation, the majority of whom will be living in urban areas, will judge us by whether we were asking the right questions today about their urban environments. They will want to know whether we funded the right research to address those questions. And they will also want to know whether we used the research findings wisely.

Notes

1. M. Gordon Wolman, "Population, Land Use, and Environment: A Long History," in *Population and Land Use in Developing Countries*, ed. Carole L. Jolly and Barbara Boyle Torrey, Committee on Population, Commission on Behavioral and Social Sciences and Education, National Research Council (Washington, DC: National Academies Press, 1993).

2. United Nations, *World Urbanization Prospects: The 2003 Revision* (New York: UN, 2004).

3. World Bank, *World Development Report 2002: Building Institutions for Markets* (New York: Oxford University Press for the World Bank, 2002).

4. Nathan Keyfitz, "Impact of Trends in Resources, Environment and Development on Demographic Prospects," in *Population and Resources in a Changing World*, ed. Kingsley Davis et al. Stanford, CA: Morrison Institute for Population and Resource Studies, 1989).

5. United Nations, *World Urbanization Prospects*.

6. National Research Council, *Cities Transformed: Demographic Change and Its Implications in the Developing World*, ed. Mark R. Montgomery et al., Panel on Urban Population Dynamics, Committee on Population, Commission on Behavioral and Social Sciences and Education, National Research Council (Washington, DC: National Academies Press, 2003).

7. United Nations, *World Urbanization Prospects*: 193.

8. Martin Brockerhoff, "Fertility and Family Planning in African Cities: The Impact of Female Migration," *Journal of Biosocial Science* 27, no. 3 (1995): 347–58; and Robert Gardner and Richard Blackburn, "People Who Move: New Reproductive Health

Focus," *Population Reports* Vol. 24, no. 3 (Baltimore, MD: Johns Hopkins School of Public Health, Population Information Program, November 1996).

9. Estimates calculated from 90 Demographic and Health Surveys as reported in National Research Council, *Cities Transformed: Demographic Change and Its Implications in the Developing World*.

10. Jyoti K. Parikh et al., Indira Gandhi Institute of Development Research, "Consumption Patterns: The Driving Force of Environmental Stress" (presented at the United Nations Conference on Environment and Development, August 1991).

11. Jeffrey R. Taylor and Karen A. Hardee, *Consumer Demand in China: A Statistical Factbook* (Boulder, CO: Westview Press, 1986): 112.

12. Taylor and Hardee, *Consumer Demand in China*: 148.

13. US Census Bureau, *Statistical Abstract of the United States: 2003* (Washington, DC: Government Printing Office, 2003).

14. Taylor and Hardee, *Consumer Demand in China*: 125.

15. Gretchen Kolsrud and Barbara Boyle Torrey, "The Importance of Population Growth in Future Commercial Energy Consumption," in *Global Climate Change: Linking Energy, Environment, Economy and Equity*, ed. James C. White (New York: Plenum Press, 1992): 127–42.

16. Andrew S. Goudie, *The Human Impact on the Natural Environment*, 2d ed. (Cambridge, MA: MIT Press, 1987): 263.

17. Goudie, *The Human Impact on the Natural Environment*: 265.

18. Kolsrud and Torrey, "The Importance of Population Growth in Future Commercial Energy Consumption": 268.

19. Martin Brockerhoff and Ellen Brennan, "The Poverty of Cities in Developing Regions," *Population and Development Review* 24, no. 1 (March 1998): 75–114.

20. Eugene Linden, "The Exploding Cities of the Developing World," *Foreign Affairs* 75, no. 1 (1996): 52–65.

21. Organisation of Economic Co-operation and Development (OECD), *Better Understanding Our Cities, The Role of Urban Indicators* (Paris: OECD, 1997).

22. Ismail Serageldin, Richard Barrett, and Joan Martin-Brown, "The Business of Sustainable Cities," *Environmentally Sustainable Development Proceedings Series*, no. 7 (Washington, DC: The World Bank, 1994).

23. Serageldin, Barrett, and Martin-Brown, "The Business of Sustainable Cities": 33.

> "*Specialization made farms less resilient: If a key crop failed or prices tumbled, they had no other income source. Most farmers stopped growing their own food, which made them dependent on agribusiness retailers.*"

Regenerative Agriculture Can Make Farmers Stewards of the Land Again

Stephanie Anderson

In the following viewpoint, Stephanie Anderson argues that the biggest challenge faced by farmers is climate change. The author explains that farmers have been focused on changing conventional methods of farming in favor of sustainability, which doesn't adequately address challenges brought on by climate change. She notes that the methods of regenerative agriculture can restore resources. However, many farmers are penned in by the United States' current agriculture system, which has been harmful not only for small farmers but also for the environment. Anderson is an instructor of English at Florida Atlantic University. She is the author of One Size Fits None: A Farm Girl's Search for the Promise of Regenerative Agriculture.

As you read, consider the following questions:

1. Why did small farms consolidate into large ones in the previous century?
2. How does regenerative agriculture make farmers less dependent on agribusiness products?
3. How does embracing the environment instead of fighting it lead to success, according to the farmer quoted in the viewpoint?

For years, "sustainable" has been the buzzword in conversations about agriculture. If farmers and ranchers could slow or stop further damage to land and water, the thinking went, that was good enough. I thought that way too, until I started writing my new book, *One Size Fits None: A Farm Girl's Search for the Promise of Regenerative Agriculture.*

I grew up on a cattle ranch in western South Dakota and once worked as an agricultural journalist. For me, agriculture is more than a topic—it is who I am. When I began working on my book, I thought I would be writing about sustainability as a response to the environmental damage caused by conventional agriculture—farming that is industrial and heavily reliant on oil and agrochemicals, such as pesticides and fertilizers.

But through research and interviews with farmers and ranchers around the United States, I discovered that sustainability's "give back what you take" approach, which usually just maintains or marginally improves resources already degraded by generations of conventional agriculture, does not adequately address the biggest long-term challenge farmers face: climate change.

But there is an alternative. A method called regenerative agriculture promises to create new resources, restoring them to preindustrial levels or better. This is good for farmers as well as the environment, since it lets them reduce their use of agrochemicals while making their land more productive.

What Holds Conventional Farmers Back

Modern American food production remains predominantly conventional. Growing up in a rural community of farmers and ranchers, I saw firsthand why.

As food markets globalized in the early 1900s, farmers began specializing in select commodity crops and animals to increase profits. But specialization made farms less resilient: If a key crop failed or prices tumbled, they had no other income source. Most farmers stopped growing their own food, which made them dependent on agribusiness retailers.

Under these conditions small farms consolidated into large ones as families went bankrupt—a trend that continues today. At the same time, agribusiness companies began marketing new machines and agrochemicals. Farmers embraced these tools, seeking to stay in business, specialize further and increase production.

In the 1970s, the government's position became "Get big or get out" under Earl Butz, who served as Secretary of Agriculture from 1971 to 1976. In the years since, critics like the nonprofit Food and Water Watch have raised concerns that corporate representatives have dictated land grant university research by obtaining leadership positions, funding agribusiness-friendly studies, and silencing scientists whose results conflict with industrial principles.

These companies have also shaped government policies in their favor, as economist Robert Albritton describes in his book *Let Them Eat Junk*. These actions encouraged the growth of large industrialized farms that rely on genetically modified seeds, agrochemicals and fossil fuel.

Several generations into this system, many conventional farmers feel trapped. They lack the knowledge required to farm without inputs, their farms are big and highly specialized, and most are carrying operating loans and other debts.

In contrast, regenerative agriculture releases farmers from dependence on agribusiness products. For example, instead of purchasing synthetic fertilizers for soil fertility, producers rely on diverse crop rotations, no-till planting and management of livestock grazing impacts.

Agribusiness dogma says that regenerative agriculture cannot feed the world and or ensure a healthy bottom line for farmers, even as conventional farmers are going bankrupt. I have heard this view from people I grew up with in South Dakota and interviewed as a farm journalist.

"Everybody seems to want smaller local producers," Ryan Roth, a farmer from Belle Glade, Florida told me. "But they can't keep up. It's unfortunate. I think it's not the best development for agriculture operations to get bigger, but it is what we're dealing with."

The Climate Threat

Climate change is making it increasingly hard for farmers to keep thinking this way. The United Nations Intergovernmental Panel on Climate Change (IPCC) has warned that without rapid action to reduce greenhouse gas emissions over roughly the next decade, warming will trigger devastating impacts such as wildfires, droughts, floods and food shortages.

For farmers, large-scale climate change will cause decreased crop yields and quality, heat stress for livestock, disease and pest outbreaks, desertification on rangelands, changes in water availability and soil erosion.

As I explain in my book, regenerative agriculture is an effective response to climate change because producers do not use agrochemicals—many of which are derived from fossil fuels—and greatly reduce their reliance on oil. The experiences of farmers who have adopted regenerative agriculture show that it restores soil carbon, literally locking carbon up underground, while also reversing desertification, recharging water systems, increasing biodiversity and reducing greenhouse gas emissions. And it produces nutrient-rich food and promises to enliven rural communities and reduce corporate control of the food system.

No Single Model

How farmers put this strategy into practice differs depending on their location, goals and community needs. Regenerative agriculture is a one-size-fits-none model of farming that allows for flexibility and close tailoring to individual environments.

At Great Plains Buffalo in South Dakota, for example, rancher Phil Jerde is reversing desertification on the grassland. Phil moves buffalo across the land in a way that mimics their historic movement over the Great Plains, rotating them frequently through small pastures so they stay bunched together and impact the land evenly via their trampling and waste distribution. The land has adequate time to rest and regrow between rotations.

After transitioning his conventional ranch to a regenerative one over 10 years, Phil saw bare ground revert back to prairie grassland. Water infiltration into the ground increased, his herd's health improved, wildlife and insect populations recovered and native grasses reappeared.

On Brown's Ranch in North Dakota, farmer Gabe Brown also converted his conventional operation to a regenerative one in a decade. He used a combination of cover crops, multicropping (growing two or more crops on a piece of land in a single season), intercropping (growing two or more crops together), an intensive rotational grazing system called mob grazing, and no-till farming to restore soil organic matter levels to just over 6 percent—roughly the level most native prairie soils contained before settlers plowed them up. Restoring organic matter sequesters carbon in the soil, helping to slow climate change.

Conventional farmers often worry about losing the illusion of control that agrochemicals, monocultures and genetically modified seeds provide. I asked Gabe how he overcame these fears. He replied that one of the most important lessons was learning to embrace the environment instead of fighting it.

"Regenerative agriculture can be done anywhere because the principles are the same," he said. "I always hear, 'We don't get the moisture or this or that.' The principles are the same everywhere. There's nature everywhere. You're just mimicking nature is all you're doing."

The Future

Researchers with Project Drawdown, a nonprofit that spotlights substantive responses to climate change, estimate that land devoted to regenerative agriculture worldwide will increase from 108 million acres currently to 1 billion acres by 2050. More resources are appearing to help farmers make the transition, such as investment groups, university programs and farmer-to-farmer training networks.

Organic food sales continue to rise, suggesting that consumers want responsibly grown food. Even big food companies like General Mills are embracing regenerative agriculture.

The question now is whether more of America's farmers and ranchers will do the same.

Periodical and Internet Sources Bibliography

The following articles have been selected to supplement the diverse views presented in this chapter.

Abdishakur, "Land Use/Land Cover Classification with Deep Learning," Towards Data Science, August 24, 2018. https:// towardsdatascience.com/land-use-land-cover-classification-with -deep-learning-9a5041095ddb.

Economist, "Trees Are Covering More of the Land in Rich Countries," November 30, 2017. https://www.economist.com/international /2017/11/30/trees-are-covering-more-of-the-land-in-rich -countries?zid=313&ah=fe2aac0b11adef572d67aed9273b6e55.

Joyce Etim, "Land Use: Definition and Different Types of Land Use," JotScroll, March 7, 2018. http://www.jotscroll.com/forums/3 /posts/204/land-use-definition-6-types-of-land-use.html.

Carlo Fezzi, "The Environmental Impact of Climate Change Adaptation on Land Use and Water Quality," *Nature,* February 16, 2015. https://www.nature.com/articles/nclimate2525.

Sandy Ikeda, "Shut Out: How Land-Use Regulations Hurt the Poor," Foundation for Economic Education, February 5, 2015. https://fee .org/articles/shut-out-how-land-use-regulations-hurt-the-poor.

Carey Island, "A Recipe for Sustainability," *Economist,* July 30, 2015. https://www.economist.com/business/2015/07/30/a-recipe-for -sustainability.

Paul Krugman, "Why Can't We Get Cities Right?" *New York Times,* September 4, 2017. https://www.nytimes.com/2017/09/04 /opinion/houston-harvey-infrastructure-development.html.

Adam Matthews, "The Environmental Crisis in Your Closet," *Newsweek,* August 13, 2015. https://www.newsweek.com /2015/08/21/environmental-crisis-your-closet-362409.html.

Martin Mowforth, "Indigenous People and the Crisis over Land and Resources," *Guardian,* September 23, 2014. https://www .theguardian.com/global-development/2014/sep/23/indigenous -people-crisis-land-resources.

Nancy Thompson, "Land Use Classifications Can Vary with Your Needs," Useful Community Development. https://www.useful -community-development.org/land-use-classifications.html.

OPPOSING
VIEWPOINTS®
SERIES

Does the Negative Impact of Development on the Environment Outweigh Its Benefits?

Chapter Preface

L and development undoubtedly has an effect on the environment. Is it all positive or negative? The answer, of course, is more complex. While land development can have tremendous benefits, such as growth of crops to feed a growing population or development of urban neighborhoods to meet the needs of city dwellers, it also can harm the environment.

For all its importance, agriculture also has contributed to the depletion of the environment. Large plantations and industrial farms in particular have driven out species from their native habitats, polluted water supplies, and contributed to flooding. They also have negatively affected local populations and in some cases have resulted in displacement of native peoples.

But it doesn't have to be that way. Sustainable agriculture practices can mitigate many of these negative impacts. Some experts argue that sustainable agriculture can even improve the environment. Worldwide commissions recommend an increase of small-scale farms and greater oversight of larger farms. The support of fair trade goods also encourages sustainable land management while also keeping native peoples on their land and continuing their way of life.

Humans have an impact on the land and the environment, but the negative aspects can be minimized with careful planning and oversight. Land is a valuable resource for any nation. It is up to the nation's leaders to decide how it is used to best contribute to economic development.

> *"Large-scale investments in agriculture do not necessarily increase food supply, close yield gaps or expand production. Rather, such investments often negatively affect local populations, leading to dispossession and displacement."*

International Investments in Agriculture Can Negatively Affect Local Populations

Pablo Pacheco

In the following viewpoint, Pablo Pacheco argues that large-scale foreign investments in agriculture do not necessarily increase food supply, expand production, or close yield gaps. The author states that such investments often negatively affect local populations and lead to dispossession and displacement. He contends that large-scale investments in plantations often undermine food security, damage local livelihoods, and reduce access to key resources. Promises of employment often do not materialize, and people from outside the area often take the few jobs that are created. Pacheco is senior scientist at the Center for International Forestry Research.

"The Negative Impacts Can Outweigh the Benefits in International Investments in Agriculture," by Pablo Pacheco, Center for International Forestry Research, January 28, 2012. Reprinted by permission.

As you read, consider the following questions:

1. About how much land in middle- and low-income countries have international investors acquired, according the UN report cited in this viewpoint?
2. Why are large-scale plantations the most common form for these foreign investments?
3. Why do the authors of the report recommend enhancing the capacity of smallholders?

A trend in recent years of international investors snapping up land in developing countries for agriculture has captured the attention of academics, policymakers, media and civil society groups. Their interpretations of the possible implications vary, due as much to ideology as to evidence. Defenders emphasise that foreign investments contribute towards overcoming technological constraints, fostering agricultural modernisation and linking local economies with global markets. Critics highlight concerns about equitable access to food, protection of local tenure rights and enhanced benefit-sharing from land development. For their part, environmentalists often have mixed feelings: on the one hand, investors are seen as among the main players causing forest destruction, but on the other hand, they are also perceived as having an important role to play in conservation.

International investment in agriculture in developing countries, which prompts large-scale land appropriation, is not a new trend but it has new connotations. Thus, understanding its dynamics in order to devise effective policy responses to manage the impacts constitutes an urgent task—and a difficult one. Multiple drivers shape investments in land and agriculture. These investments involve a diverse number of actors (from international to local) that often have different motivations (production or speculation); their impacts, too, are diverse, depending on the specific local conditions where these investments take place. Shedding light on their magnitude and social, economic and environmental outcomes

Benefits of Sustainable Development

Agriculture takes a heavy toll on the health of the environment through agricultural runoff and some farming practices. Sustainable development in agriculture focuses on ways to reduce these impacts through better management practices.

Farmers can accomplish this in several ways. One way they can do this is through Integrated Pest Management or IPM. By minimizing fertilizer and pesticide use, farmers can protect their land and adjacent lands from their effects. Famers can practice crop or grazing plot rotation to reduce the effects of soil erosion and nonpoint source pollution from runoff. The farmer and the environment benefit from the preservation of topsoil.

Likewise, forestry practices can create sustainable resources through planned harvest and avoidance of clear-cutting. Rotation of sun-tolerant and intolerant species can ensure the land and soil are protected. Sustainable development of forests recognizes that trees provide environmental benefits that go beyond timber harvesting.

It recognizes that the biological diversity of forests must be maintained in order to protect the health of the ecosystem. It acknowledges the forests' role in carbon dioxide sequestration, the process of removal and storage of atmospheric carbon dioxide in trees and other vegetation.

Ecotourism fosters sustainable development by helping local populations see the value of their natural resources. This type of tourism practices minimal impact and an approach to building environmental awareness in local communities and ecotourists.

Local populations receive direct financial benefits from their natural resources, which empower them and give them the knowledge to make informed decisions regarding their environment. Ecotourists, in turn, take back this message of sustainable development.

The question of how sustainable development affects the environment is dependent upon knowledge. With knowledge of the value of the natural resources as well as the consequence of their destruction can people realize the impact of their choices. In this way, the environment will maintain its health and vitality for future generations.

"Sustainable Development for Affecting Environments Positively," by Rebecca Scudder, Bright Hub Inc., September 4, 2011.

is fundamental if effective policy responses are to be devised, not only to reduce their negative impacts but also to enhance their positive contributions.

With this aim, the UN Committee on World Food Security's High Level Panel of Experts on Food Security and Nutrition produced a report on this issue. The authors, Toulmin and colleagues, analysed available estimates and found that international investors have acquired about 50–80 million hectares of land in middle- and low-income countries, through either purchases or lease agreements. Two-thirds of this area is in sub-Saharan Africa. The authors reiterate what is generally already known about the drivers shaping this trend: the rise in investments is largely associated with growing demand for food, feed, fibre and biofuels, as well as financial speculation. Multiple interests are involved in making these deals possible—from corporate firms at the international level, to local authorities, entrepreneurs and government officials at the local level. While the report acknowledges that national investors play an important role in the agricultural sector, its focus is on large-scale international investments.

Toulmin and colleagues suggest that large-scale investments in agriculture do not necessarily increase food supply, close yield gaps or expand production. Rather, such investments often negatively affect local populations, leading to dispossession and displacement. The authors indicate that land appropriation by firms often takes place through leases (because, in many cases, national governments do not permit foreigners to own land) or through states handing local people's land to large-scale commercial investors based on the concept of "eminent domain." The terms of the contracts and compensations for local populations are highly questionable.

While these investments could take different forms, large-scale plantations are the most common result. Toulmin and colleagues argue that this model tends to dominate because governments are offering investments in large tracts of land rather than promoting more inclusive business models, such as contract farming. The authors conclude that large-scale investments in plantations often damage local livelihoods, undermine food security and reduce access to key resources. Promises of employment often do not materialise and people from outside the area often take the few jobs created. Furthermore, farmland acquisitions have significant gender implications because women encounter systematic discrimination with regard to access and decision-making, as well as ownership and control of land. Finally, the authors indicate that the direct and indirect negative impacts are relatively severe because of pressures on forest conversion, soil erosion and water pollution. Nonetheless, a range of possible outcomes may result from different combinations of land security, regulations and market conditions.

The report describes many governance initiatives emerging at different levels, and with different aims and scopes, to address the socio-economic and environmental impacts of large-scale investments. These include voluntary guidelines, industry-based roundtables and changes in national policies related to issues such as tenure, the environment and taxation. The report ends with a list of recommendations for each type of actor.

Overall, the report makes a good case for stronger action at multiple levels and for the involvement of multiple stakeholders in order to improve the governance and oversight of international investments, mainly to ameliorate their observed negative impacts. Further opportunities exist for better understanding of how the proposed policy responses (and the incentives they engender) may realistically work in the various settings under which large-scale land acquisitions occur. Moreover, while the authors suggest ways to enhance the capacity of smallholders, harnessing existing potential can do much. A multitude of small-scale resource management systems can reconcile social, economic and environmental goals. Therefore, enhancing governance of large-scale investments and supporting the potential of smallholders emerge as global priorities to be pursued in concert.

> *"Sustainable management of our land
> can help restore soil fertility, prevent
> water pollution and decrease the
> amount of greenhouse gas emissions
> from this important economic sector."*

Sustainable Agriculture Can Actually Restore the Environment

Greentumble

In the following viewpoint, authors from Greentumble argue that although agricultural practices can—and have—depleted the land in much of the world, it doesn't have to be that way. The authors contend that agriculture can restore the land rather than harm it. Sustainable agriculture practices such as government programs, land management such as prescribed burning and crop rotation, and rotational livestock grazing systems can all help encourage a healthy environment and ecosystem development while also yielding hearty crops. Greentumble is an online resource that promotes a more sustainable lifestyle.

As you read, consider the following questions:

1. How can agriculture sequester carbon?
2. What are some examples of perennial plants grown on farms that can help prevent flooding and reduce water pollution?
3. How has urban farming helped the environment, according to the viewpoint?

Historical civilizations and modern life, as we know it, would not have been possible without agriculture. It was through the cultivation of nutritional sources of food that the structure of early societies could diversify and focus on various tasks. Without the need to move to better hunting grounds or spend time on dangerous quests after seasonal sources of food dissipated, early humans were able to settle and use their energy towards manufacturing sophisticated tools and building permanent dwellings.

As time passed, agriculture became the most dominant land use on the planet, feeding a booming population, while accounting for 70% of the world's freshwater withdrawals, as well as reducing the natural habitat of 53% of threatened terrestrial species.[1] Regardless of farming methods, agriculture alters the original ecosystem and thus affects the environment.

Whether this change has come with negative or positive consequences depends largely only on our approach, because agriculture can have positive effects on the environment when done sustainably. Sustainable management of our land can help restore soil fertility, prevent water pollution and decrease the amount of greenhouse gas emissions from this important economic sector.

You may think it sounds counter-intuitive, but keep on reading if you want to learn how our involvement in agricultural activities can actually restore the environment instead of depleting our natural resources.

How Does Agriculture Benefit Our Environment?
Agriculture Inspires People

Farmers have shaped and maintained the unique look of rural areas for millennia. Farms create wonderful variety of landscapes, ranging from beautiful blossoming orchards and vineyards to fields of golden wheat. And it is not only the 45.7% of people worldwide that live in the countryside[2] that enjoy it, but the rest of population living in urban areas enjoy agricultural landscapes as a place to reconnect with nature. This way agriculture encourages people to interact with nature in a positive way, inspiring them to conserve it.

Agriculture Preserves Ecosystems

Agriculture helps preserve valuable ecosystems. A perfect example is the extensive farming of increasingly rare permanent grasslands in Romania. Grasslands provide habitat to a great number of animals and native plants. These areas have been almost entirely wiped out in other countries of Europe due to modern development or intensive agriculture. In Romania, however, they still exist because of the traditional (low-impact) way of farming and seasonal grazing of livestock by shepherds.

Both methods naturally maintain and enrich these habitats, promoting healthy regrowth of unique high-biodiversity vegetation. The importance of these grasslands has been recognized by the European Union, and the concept of High Nature Value farmland was created to provide incentives for farmers to protect these areas and manage them accordingly.[3]

Other examples from our daily life are fair trade goods. Fair trade chocolate and coffee from rainforests encourages sustainable management of rainforests from where these goods originate. Fair trade also helps native people retain their traditional ways of life in a way that works in harmony with local ecosystems and gives incentives to continue to protect them.[4]

Agriculture Creates Habitats

Agricultural systems that work in harmony with nature such as organic, permaculture, or biodynamic farming create diverse natural habitats. For example, open meadow habitats are important for species like waterfowl, amphibians, and for pollinators.

Some species even increase in number due to agricultural activities. One such species is the North American White-tailed Deer (Odocoileus virginianus), which does very well in open farm field habitat.

Maintaining land for agricultural use can also prevent that land from being developed and urbanized, in areas where native species have difficulty finding original habitat. For this purpose, the United States Department of Agriculture Farm Service Agency (FSA) created seven voluntary land conservation programs. One of them offers yearly payment to farmers for not cultivating land with high environmental value. The Conservation Reserve Program (CRP) is aimed at protecting native species and conserving soils by taking the land out of agricultural production.

Agriculture Sets Back Ecological Succession

Some species need early successional habitats, such as prairies, to thrive. These habitats are highly ephemeral and can be identified by vigorously growing grasses, forbs, shrubs and trees but which need disturbance to be maintained.[9] Open meadow habitats, which fall under this category, and native wildflowers are important for many pollinators like some birds and bees. Without farmland, succession may need to be deliberately set back by management activities, such as prescribed burning, to help early successional species survive.

Intentional burning was one of the primary ways that native people managed the landscape in North America prior to European settlement in order to provide for their own agricultural and hunting activities.[5]

Agriculture Boosts Soil Fertility

One of the key features of sustainable farming is the focus on the health of soils. Practices such as crop rotation, cover cropping, no-tillage and the application of compost, improve soil fertility naturally and can even speed up the process of new topsoil formation. In addition to preventing the exhaustion of soils, and therefore, helping secure stable yields, these practices increase biodiversity of favorable soil fauna and flora.

Soils rich in organic matter and flourishing with life also contain greater concentrations of the natural enemies of pests, thus supporting the growth of more resilient crops. According to Dr. Elaine Ingham, one teaspoon of healthy soil can contain up to 1 billion helpful bacteria, while concentration in intensively farmed soils might drop to one hundred.[6]

Agriculture Sequesters Carbon

As with any other plants, growing crops, especially in perennial polyculture systems, used in permaculture farming and agroforestry, adds oxygen to the atmosphere as plants photosynthesize and remove carbon dioxide from the atmosphere. The richer the plant cover is, the more it uses carbon dioxide to support its life functions.

Carbon is also sequestered by soils, which have a natural carbon carrying capacity that increases when soils are managed with minimum disturbance.

> For example, the Center for Climate and Energy Solutions states that U.S. arable soils currently sequester 20 million metric tons of carbon per year and their full potential can be up to 7 times higher, if some soil conservation practices were applied.[7]

Interestingly, carbon can be reduced even by a livestock farm. In rotational grazing systems, animals help to store carbon in the soil. Through grazing for a limited time period in one area, biodiversity of native plants increases because grasses have time to regrow equally without one species taking over and becoming invasive. Richer and better quality pasture means more organic material entering soils, which makes soils healthy and increases their capacity to sequester carbon from the atmosphere.[8]

Agriculture Retains Soil and Prevents Erosion

Loss of soils is one of the biggest threats to our wellbeing, and intensive agriculture with monoculture fields is known to be one of its main contributors. Farmers, however, have the ability to reverse this damage.

In perennial systems, vegetation with deep roots helps to hold the soil together and prevent erosion. This is especially the case when farmers have constructed swales and other types of earthworks that help to stabilize steep slopes, or when applying techniques with low soil disturbance such as no-tillage.

Agriculture Has a Role in the Water Cycle

Plants and trees in agricultural systems help to retain and add water to underground aquifers. This process is most effective when the crops being grown are perennials that continue to grow every year and have deep, well-established root systems.

A successful strategy that has been applied already by our ancestors is to plant trees, bushes and grasses mixed together. By combining plants of different sizes, soils are evenly covered and can withstand torrential rains without being washed away. This improves soil structure and enables rainwater infiltration. Once water enters the soil, it passes through different soil layers all the time getting rid of pollutants until it reaches groundwater reservoirs perfectly clean and safe for us to drink.

Examples of some perennial plants grown on farms are alfalfa, fruit trees, olive trees, berries and grapes. Together, they act as an important buffer in the landscape, preventing flooding, reducing water pollution from agricultural runoff and preventing erosion, while providing us with nutritious food at the same time.

Agriculture Can Conserve Water

Farming practices such as strip or no-till, dry farming and planting of cover crops significantly reduce the need to irrigate. According to researchers from UC Davis, cover crops such as rye on organic farms are able to retain 50% more rainwater and reduce surface runoff by 35%. The higher the water content in the soil, the less irrigation is needed during dry spells to preserve crops, which saves significant amounts of water over the long term.

In certain forms of agriculture, properly processed sewage, wastewater, and sludge can be used on the landscape instead of disposing it as waste. In these cases, wisely chosen vegetation acts as a "living filter," getting rid of pollutants, while utilizing water for growing. This method saves farmers money, conserves water, and recycles nutrients.

Agriculture Provides Food from Limited Sources

Urban agriculture on a small scale can help to localize food production, reducing the overall environmental footprint of our modern food systems. Benefits include lower greenhouse gas emissions, minimal transportation requirements, and reduced energy use for food production.

As the benefits are becoming more and more acknowledged, the trend of urban farming is starting to become quite popular. Besides connecting people together and with nature, urban farms supply food to about 700 million city dwellers. And by achieving maximum use of available resources, an area of one square meter can produce up to 20kg of food each year.

Aren't these perfect arguments for how great agriculture can be, if we only switched to more ecologically-friendly methods and returned to a chemical-free approach? It is our collective responsibility to eliminate negative impacts of food production and focus on achieving balance between the land's productivity and the preservation of natural habitats.

Notes

1. https://goo.gl/rLARnk

2. http://data.worldbank.org/indicator/SP.RUR.TOTL.ZS?end=2016&start=2016&view=bar

3. https://goo.gl/U8xHgH

4. http://www.rainforest-alliance.org/

5. http://www.californiachaparral.com/enativeamericans.html

6. https://www.thebalance.com/environmental-benefits-of-organic-farming-2538317

7. https://www.c2es.org/publications/agricultures-role-addressing-climate-change#.3

8. https://goo.gl/y9HyNy

9. https://goo.gl/Aw1m9M

> *"It is, therefore, important that people make proper and sustainable use of their natural resources so that they can also be preserved, to some extent, for posterity."*

Natural Resources Have Tremendous Potential to Accelerate Economic Development

Help Save Nature

In the following viewpoint, authors from Help Save Nature argue that a country's natural resources can contribute a great deal to a country's economic development. Therefore, the way a country uses its land is very important. Development of land in a way that is unsustainable may deplete important resources and result in economic stagnation or worse. It is important for a country's government to make a strong commitment to its natural resources as well as its management of them. Help Save Nature is an online resource that increases public awareness about environmental problems and promotes solutions to fix them.

"How Do Natural Resources Affect Economic Development?" by Help Save Nature, Buzzle.com, March 26, 2018. Reprinted by permission.

As you read, consider the following questions:

1. What is the goal of economic development for any country?
2. What is one example of a nonrenewable resource?
3. Why do an abundance of natural resources not always translate to economic well-being for a country's citizens?

The term *economic development* refers to the kind of advancement made by a particular economy, both qualitatively as well as quantitatively, in a given period of time. Economic growth in terms of rise in market productivity as well as in the overall GDP is an important aspect of economic development, alongside many others. But, the ultimate aim of development of any economy across the world is to ensure the economic and social well-being of the people. There are numerous players determining the economic development of a country or region, the most important of which, alongside the physical capital, is its human capital, or in simple terms, the manpower resources. Apart from these two, economists from across the globe have acknowledged the vital role that is played in the economic development by, what they term as the natural capital, or what we, in simple terms, may refer to as natural resources.

What Are Natural Resources?

Natural resources are those material and substances, which occur naturally in the environment. They are those resources that are readily and naturally available on our planet, and can be used in their natural, undisturbed form. Some of the common examples of natural resources include land, water, coal, wood, sunlight, and oil.

All these resources are distributed randomly across our planet, owing to which, every place has a set of its own natural resources, which aid in its economic development. Because these resources are randomly distributed, they are available in abundance in some places, whereas they are found in scarcity in some others. It is, therefore, important that people make proper and sustainable use of their natural resources so that they can also be preserved, to some extent, for posterity. Natural resources have been essentially classified into two types:

The non-renewable resources are those natural resources, which can be used only once. They are exhaustible resources, which tend to diminish in quantity, owing to their constant usage. It is, hence, important to use the non-renewable resources wisely so that we do not run out of them. Non-renewable resources include coal, natural gas, petroleum, uranium, etc.

The renewable resources are those natural resources, which can be naturally restored. While some of these resources are available in plenty everywhere and at all times, like wind, sunlight, etc., some other renewable resources, such as timber and water require time to be replenished. So, if these resources are used up at a faster pace than the time taken by nature to restore them, even they are prone to getting exhausted.

Several economists of the world have observed that the availability of abundant natural resources, whether renewable or non-renewable, in a particular region, accelerates the economic development therein. However, it should be noted that the use and exploitation of the natural resources depends on the attitude of the people of a particular region, and hence, the above observation has also been seen to be reversed in some cases.

Impact of Natural Resources on Economic Development

Natural resources are available, in varying quantities, in all parts of the world. The natural availability of certain resources in a given region, makes it easier for the people to acquire and use them. Otherwise, a country, where a certain natural resource is not available, has to depend on other countries, in order to acquire it, owing to which the former has to invest a lot of monetary resources in the trade.

Environmental Impact Analysis

An environmental impact analysis is typically conducted to assess the potential impact a proposed development project will have on the natural and social environment. This may include an assessment of both the short- and long-term effects on the physical environment, such as air, water and/or noise pollution; as well as effects on local services, living and health standards, and aesthetics.

In enacting the National Environmental Policy Act (NEPA) of 1969, Congress required all agencies of the Federal government to give equal consideration to environmental consequences as well as to economic motivations and technological feasibility when making a decision that could affect the quality of the human and natural environment. NEPA also established the Council on Environmental Quality within the Executive Office of the President to ensure that federal agencies would meet their obligations under the Act.

One provision of the law requires that an Environmental Impact Statement (EIS) be written for major federal actions and made available to all, including to the general public. An EIS must include: the environmental impacts of a proposed action; unavoidable adverse environmental impacts; alternatives—including no action; the relationship between short-term uses of the environment and maintenance of long-term ecological productivity; irreversible and

The effect that the availability of natural resources may or may not have on the economic development of a country, depends on various parameters. As economist, Sir William Arthur Lewis puts it, "Given the country's resources, its rate of growth is determined by human behavior and human institutions: by such things as energy of mind, the attitude towards material things, willingness to save and invest productively or the freedom and flexibility of institutions."

However, for the common people of a country to be aware of the value of natural resources, it is extremely vital that the political structures are strong enough. If a country is fortunate irretrievable commitments of resources; and secondary/cumulative effects of implementing the proposed action. Now, most state and local governments also require that environmental impact analyses be conducted prior to any major development projects.

Environmental impact analyses are often challenging because they call for making projections with incomplete information. Methods of assessing the impacts typically include both objective and subjective information making it difficult to quantify. Therefore, the methods are frequently seen as complex and, oftentimes, controversial. Despite being a requirement for many development projects, the function of an environmental impact statement is merely procedural. There is no specific legal force of action if information stemming from an environmental impact analysis confirms that a particular project may harm the environment. As a result, it is often left up to the courts to rule on whether risks to the environment are overstated or not.

Although an environmental impact analysis often raises more questions than it answers as it examines the various links between social, economic, technological, and ecological factors involved in a potential development project, it also provides a practical and interesting approach to the understanding and appreciation of the many complexities and uncertainties involved with these interrelationships.

"Environmental Impact Analysis," The Environmental Literacy Council.

enough to have a good leadership, the attitude of the common masses can be mended in a way that they learn to use their natural resources wisely and in a sustainable manner. So, whether or not the country's reserve of natural resources actually aids in its economic development is determined largely, by the quality of public response, rather than the amount of resources.

Having said this, the link between the availability of natural resources and overall economic development may not indeed be as strong as it is often perceived. After all, we do have examples of several countries, which have remarkably risen to development, despite having scarce amounts of natural resources, and even hostile environmental conditions. Japan is a classic example of this. On the other hand, we also have instances, wherein no remarkable progress has been made by a nation, in spite of having enormous reserves of natural resources. Take for example, the African countries of Congo, Angola, and Gabon. These countries have unparalleled reserves of natural resources, yet extreme poverty is what prevails amongst majority of their masses.

The Developing Country Scenario

- It is important to note that in a developing economy, natural resources can provide a number of opportunities, in order to enhance the economic development.
- In an agrarian economy, for instance, natural resources, such as land, soil, forests, animals, fisheries, etc., may be extremely important.
- These not only maintain the livelihood of the people, but also provide them with subsistence.
- Therefore, it becomes very necessary to keep a check on the use of these resources, as even if some of them, like land may be renewable, the law of diminishing returns still applies.

The Developed Country Scenario

- Contrary to the developing countries, natural resources may not occupy a prominent place in the process of economic development of the developed countries.
- Developed countries are technologically advanced, and hence, even if there is a scarcity of some natural resource, say cultivable land, they can still produce enormous amount of crop using sophisticated technology.
- Therefore, technology and capital overshadows the need for natural resources in the economic development of these countries.
- Owing to this, the law of diminishing returns rarely applies to the natural resources of the developed countries. As the

economist, Sir Henry Roy Forbes Harrod has said, "I propose to discard the law of diminishing returns from land as a primary determinant in a progressive economy. ... I discard it only because in our particular context it appears that its influence may be quantitatively unimportant."

While natural resources may be considered as one of the factors aiding the process of economic development, it needs to be noted that their excessive exploitation and/or misuse, may also hinder the same. It is, therefore, essential that economies make optimum and judicious use of their natural resources. Though it is true that mineral industries have created many jobs throughout the world, it is also vital to take note of the environmental hazards and challenges that their excessive and unethical use may pose.

> *"We are finding that there may
> be really strong signatures where
> the impact of landscape change
> occurs and they seem to be affected
> differently by human activity or by
> climate change."*

Human Impact on the Land Can Be Studied and Adjusted

Science Daily

In the following viewpoint, Science Daily reports on a ten-year project conducted by researchers from Arizona State University that studies the long-term effects humans have had on the land. The researchers argue that their method of controlled experiments, studying the past as well as the present, and computer modeling help them understand how people interact with the environment, in a field called socio-ecological science. Successful predictions of the future will help farmers see the impacts of their interactions with the land and adjust their practices as necessary. Science Daily is an online science news resource that offers breaking news about the latest scientific discoveries.

"Long-Term Study Shows Impact of Humans on Land," ScienceDaily.com, January 27, 2016. Reprinted by permission.

As you read, consider the following questions:

1. How did new computational techniques aid the researchers in their study?
2. What kind of land users were the focus of the research?
3. Why were the findings on thresholds significant?

Humans have been working the land to sustain our lives for millennia, cultivating plants or herding animals. This has created socio-ecological systems and landscapes that are a product of both human actions and natural forces.

Now researchers from Arizona State University are reporting on a 10-year project that studies the long-term effects humans have had on the land—and the consequences for the communities whose livelihoods depend on the land. Their research has led to some surprising reasons why communities survive or fail.

The work, according to Michael Barton, a professor in Arizona State University's School of Human Evolution and Social Change, provides "new insights that we don't get just from looking at the world today or even doing the normal study of the world in the past. New computational techniques let us take a long term view of socio-ecological systems and how they change over time."

Barton is the lead author of the paper, "Experimental socioecology: Integrative science for Anthropocene landscape dynamics," published in early online issue of *Anthropocene*. The paper reports on the findings from the Mediterranean Landscape Dynamics Project (MedLand), a National Science Foundation supported project that has been studying human interaction with the land in the Mediterranean region since 2004.

Barton and his colleagues, who come from a variety of scientific disciplines and several institutions, combine computer modeling with field research to understand how human and natural forces, like climate, began to interact to create socio-ecological landscapes, like terraced fields, orchards and pastures found throughout the Mediterranean today.

The focus of the research has been on small-holder farmers or herders, which still comprise more than 70 percent of the world's food producers, and how they transform landscapes over long periods of time.

"Our work focuses on how human action, even the kind of farming and herding that is not industrial scale, can have really big effects," Barton said. "The research helps us to understand the delicate balance between working the land successfully and altering the land to the point where it can no longer support us."

Among the findings, Barton said, was the idea that there are thresholds in the impacts of farming that separate success from failure. Farmers and herders can find a balance in working the land that keeps it productive. But as communities grow they may pass unforeseen thresholds where the land-use practices that once allowed them to thrive begin to destroy the productivity of the land that supports them.

"Go beyond the threshold and everything goes south," Barton said. "Continuing to do the same things that were successful in grandfather's day produces increasing problems today."

Another finding may explain why most people who produce our food either put most of their effort into cultivating crops or into herding animals. Modeling experiments show that while farmers or herders can be successful, those who try to do an equal amount of both eventually fail.

"What happens is when the population starts to grow the people who are 50/50 expand operations, but then they have dramatic crashes and sometimes never recover," Barton explained. "It looks like people who are half and half farming and herding are not practicing a sustainable way of life over the long term. It also explains why the world is divided into people who produce our food by mostly farming and who do it mostly by herding."

The research also showed how long-term small scale farming practices affect large scale, long-term environmental change in the Mediterranean.

Warnings About Unchecked Land Use

The massive conversion of the world's natural landscapes to agriculture and other human uses may soon undermine the capacity of the planet's ecosystems to sustain a burgeoning human population, according to a new report in the journal *Science*.

According to the authors, the escalating transformation of the world's forests, wetlands, savannahs, waterways and other native landscapes is the biggest potential threat to human health and global sustainability.

"Short of a collision with an asteroid, land use by humans is the most significant impact on the world's biosphere," says Jonathan A. Foley, a University of Wisconsin–Madison climatologist and lead author of the paper. "It may be the single most pressing environmental issue of our day."

According to Foley, many agricultural practices built on Western-style methods are unsustainable, requiring large applications of chemical fertilizers and further sculpting of the landscape to divert water to marginal lands.

"While land use practices vary greatly across the world, their ultimate outcome is generally the same: the acquisition of natural resources for immediate human needs, often at the expense of degrading environmental conditions," the authors write.

"What strategies can ameliorate the detrimental effects of land use?" they ask. Examples include making agricultural production more efficient; increasing green space in urban areas; employing agro-forestry practices that provide food and fiber yet maintain habitats for threatened species; and maintaining local biodiversity and associated ecosystem services, such as pollination and pest control.

"Many of these strategies involve management of landscape structure through the strategic placement of managed and natural ecosystems, so the services of natural ecosystems (e.g., pest control by natural predators, pollination by wild bees, reduced erosion with hedgerows or filtration of runoff by buffer strips) are available across the landscape mosaic," the authors note.

"Environmental Scientists Warn About the Consequences of Unchecked Land Use," by Terry Devitt and Mark Shwartz, Stanford University, July 27, 2005.

"This work has helped us differentiate between environmental changes driven by climate and environmental changes driven by human land use," Barton said. "We are finding that there may be really strong signatures where the impact of landscape change occurs and they seem to be affected differently by human activity or by climate change."

Behind all of this work is the use of an approach called experimental socio-ecology, in which computer simulations give the researchers new ways to understand how people interact with the environment.

"Using computational modeling gives us a way to carry out experiments on human environmental interactions over a long period of time," Barton explained. "More importantly, it can give us insight into the future."

He explained that the researchers compile data on farming practices, as well as soils, plant cover, climate and other aspects of the environment. They use these to create complex computer models of the impacts of different practices on landscapes. They then tune these models by seeing if they can replicate past human impacts and their consequences. A model that can "predict the past" will be more reliable at showing the potential future consequences of different farming practices in use today.

"We can run a whole series of variations on this to better understand the effects of small holder farming on the landscape at any time and at any place. We focused on the Mediterranean, but its applicable to any semi-arid landscapes," he said.

This, for Barton, is the future of understanding how humans interact with the land.

"The idea of doing these controlled experiments and contra-factual histories both of the past and of the future is, I think, a really important new way to do socio-ecological science," he said.

Periodical and Internet Sources Bibliography

*The following articles have been selected to supplement the diverse
views presented in this chapter.*

Economist, "The Long View," September 13, 2013. https://www
.economist.com/special-report/2013/09/13/the-long-view.

Environmental Protection Agency, "Land Use." https://www.epa.gov
/report-environment/land-use.

Judith Evans and Kate Allen, "Landowners Benefited from
Planning Changes, Study Shows," *Financial Times*, January 30,
2017. https://www.ft.com/content/a261cf3c-e70c-11e6-893c
-082c54a7f539.

Jaboury Ghazoul and Fritz Kleinschroth, "A Global Perspective Is
Needed to Protect Environmental Defenders," *Nature*, July 30,
2018. https://www.nature.com/articles/s41559-018-0640-1.

Nicholas Jackson, "A Conversation with Charles R. Wolfe,
Environmental Lawyer," *Atlantic*, October 3, 2011. https://www
.theatlantic.com/national/archive/2011/10/a-conversation-with
-charles-r-wolfe-environmental-lawyer/246015/.

Seema Jayachandran, "Using the Airbnb Model to Protect the
Environment," *New York Times*, December 29, 2017. https://
www.nytimes.com/2017/12/29/business/economy/airbnb
-protect-environment.html.

Edwin Loo, "The Secret of Singapore's Development Master
Plan," *Financial Times*, July 12, 2017. https://www.ft.com
/content/90409132-6626-11e7-8526-7b38dcaef614.

Raghu Murtugudde, "Global Human Population Isn't Going to
Explode—but That Doesn't Mean We're Safe," *Newsweek*,
September 26, 2018. https://www.newsweek.com/global-human
-population-explosion-carbon-emissions-consumption-1138996.

Princeton University, "Governments, Researchers Underestimate
Impact of Inefficient Land-Use on Climate Change," December
12, 2018. https://phys.org/news/2018-12-underestimate-impact
-inefficient-land-use-climate.html.

Nathan Smith, "Zoned Out," Foundation for Economic Education,
March 18, 2014. https://fee.org/articles/zoned-out.

OPPOSING
VIEWPOINTS®
SERIES

CHAPTER 3

Is Environmental Impact an Inevitable Side Effect of Land Use and Development?

Chapter Preface

How strong a correlation is there between land use and the environment? The answer only matters if global citizens and their leaders are committed to saving the planet. Choosing to engage in practices that will result in healthier land, water, and air is not always easier. It can be more expensive than the alternative, for example. It can compete with economic growth. It may not seem worth it in the short term.

The growth of cities has led to an exciting revitalization in recent decades, but overdevelopment of urban areas has had significant local impacts on weather and climate. Construction of "green" buildings and parks and a de-emphasis on auto traffic can mitigate such impacts, as can practices such as urban farming. Agriculture negatively impacts the environment in other ways, but its effects also can be limited with the proper precautions.

The mining of natural resources is key to any nation's economy. However, the methods used must be taken into consideration. When mining harms the land, alternate methods must be sought. But alternate methods are often expensive, take much longer, and drain resources in other ways.

It is essential to the health of the planet to maintain the dwindling amounts of forest land and wildnerness. In order to stop its destruction, or at the very least slow it, policies must be enacted that recognize their value. The Amazon rain forest, though in decline, has been "saved" somewhat thanks to a program enacted in Brazil that effectively protected certain areas and peoples of the rain forest, for example.

> "*Decisions about land use and land cover can therefore affect, positively or negatively, how much our climate will change and what kind of vulnerabilities humans and natural systems will face as a result.*"

Climate Adaptation Considerations Are Playing an Increasingly Large Role in Land Decisions

Daniel G. Brown and Colin Polsky

In the following excerpted viewpoint, Daniel G. Brown and Colin Polsky argue that land-use and land-cover changes affect local, regional, and global climate processes. Choices about land-use and land-cover patterns have affected and will continue to affect our vulnerability to the effects of climate change. In spite of the lack of a formal federal climate policy, climate change does seem to factor into decisions regarding changes to land use and land cover, the authors note. Brown is dean of the University of Michigan School of Natural Resources and Environment. Polsky is director of the Florida Center for Environmental Studies at Florida Atlantic University.

"Land Use and Land Cover Change," by Daniel G. Brown and Colin Polsky, US Global Change Research Program.

As you read, consider the following questions:

1. Why are cities warmer than the countryside?
2. What are three reasons why public landowners might not want to adapt their land-use methods in order to address climate change?
3. What effect does irrigation have on temperature?

In addition to emissions of heat-trapping greenhouse gases from energy, industrial, agricultural, and other activities, humans also affect climate through changes in land use (activities taking place on land, like growing food, cutting trees, or building cities) and land cover (the physical characteristics of the land surface, including grain crops, trees, or concrete). For example, cities are warmer than the surrounding countryside because the greater extent of paved areas in cities affects how water and energy are exchanged between the land and the atmosphere. This increases the exposure of urban populations to the effects of extreme heat events. Decisions about land use and land cover can therefore affect, positively or negatively, how much our climate will change and what kind of vulnerabilities humans and natural systems will face as a result.

The impacts of changes in land use and land cover cut across all regions and sectors of the National Climate Assessment. Chapters addressing each region discuss land-use and land-cover topics of particular concern to specific regions. Similarly, chapters addressing sectors examine specific land-use matters. In particular, land cover and land use are a major focus for sectors such as agriculture, forests, rural and urban communities, and Native American lands. By contrast, the key messages of this chapter are national in scope and synthesize the findings of other chapters regarding land cover and land use.

Land uses and land covers change over time in response to evolving economic, social, and biophysical conditions. Many of these changes are set in motion by individual landowners and land managers and can be quantified from satellite measurements, aerial photographs, on-the-ground observations, and reports from landowners and users., Over the past few decades, the most prominent land changes within the US have been changes in the amount and kind of forest cover due to logging practices and development in the Southeast and Northwest and to urban expansion in the Northeast and Southwest.

Because humans control land use and, to a large extent, land cover, individuals, businesses, non-profit organizations, and governments can make land decisions to adapt to and/or reduce the effects of climate change. Often the same land-use decision can serve both aims. Adaptation options (those aimed at coping with the effects of climate change) include varying the local mix of vegetation and concrete to reduce heat in cities or elevating homes to reduce exposure to sea level rise or flooding. Land-use and land-cover-related options for mitigating climate change (reducing the speed and amount of climate change) include expanding forests to accelerate removal of carbon from the atmosphere, modifying the way cities are built and organized to reduce energy and motorized transportation demands, and altering agricultural management practices to increase carbon storage in soil.

Despite this range of climate change response options, there are three main reasons why private and public landowners may choose not to modify land uses and land covers for climate adaptation or mitigation purposes. First, land decisions are influenced not only by climate but also by economic, cultural, legal, or other considerations. In many cases, climate-based land-change efforts to adapt to or reduce climate change meet with resistance because current practices are too costly to modify and/or too deeply entrenched in local societies and cultures. Second, certain land uses and land covers are simply difficult to modify, regardless of desire or intent. For instance, the number of homes constructed in floodplains or the amount of irrigated agriculture can be so deeply rooted that they are difficult to change, no matter how much those practices might impede our ability to respond to climate change. Finally, the benefits of land-use decisions made by individual landowners with specific adaptation or mitigation goals do not always accrue to those landowners or even to their communities. Therefore, without some institutional intervention (such as incentives or penalties), the motivations for such decisions can be weak.

Recent Trends

In terms of land area, the US remains a predominantly rural country, especially as its population increasingly gravitates towards urban areas. In 1910, only 46% of the US population lived in urban areas, but by 2010 that figure had climbed to more than 81%. In 2006 (the most recent year for which these data are available), more than 80% of the land cover in the lower 48 states was dominated by shrub/scrub vegetation, grasslands, forests, and agriculture. Forests and grasslands, which include acreage used for timber production and grazing, account for more than half of all US land use by area (See table on next page), about 63% of which is in private ownership, though their distribution and ownership patterns vary regionally. Agricultural land uses are carried out on 18% of US surface area. Developed or built-up areas covered only about 5% of the country's land surface, with the greatest concentrations of urban areas in the Northeast, Midwest, and Southeast. This apparently small percentage of developed area belies its rapid expansion and does not include development that is dispersed in a mosaic among other land uses (like agriculture and forests). In particular, low-density housing developments (suburban and exurban areas), which are not well-represented in commonly used satellite measurements, have rapidly expanded throughout the US over the last 60 years or so. Based on Census data, areas settled at suburban and exurban densities (1 house per 1 to 40 acres on average) cover more than 15 times the land area settled at urban densities (1 house per acre or less) and covered five times more land area in 2000 than in 1950.

Despite these rapid changes in developed land covers, the vast size of the country means that total land-cover changes in the US may appear deceptively modest. Since 1973, satellite data show that the overall rate of land-cover changes nationally has averaged about 0.33% per year. Yet this small rate of change has produced a large cumulative impact. Between 1973 and 2000, 8.6% of the area of the lower 48 states experienced land-cover change, an area roughly equivalent to the combined land area of California and Oregon.

These national-level annual rates of land changes mask considerable geographic variability in the types, rates, and causes of change. Between 1973 and 2000, the Southeast region had the highest rate of change, due to active forest timber harvesting and replanting, while the Southwest region had the lowest rate of change.

Table: Land Cover Statistics

LAND COVER CLASS	UNITED STATES
Agriculture	18.6%
Grassland, Shrub/Scrub, Moss, Lichen	39.2%
Forest	23.2%
Barren	2.6%
Developed, Built-Up	4.0%
Water, Ice, Snow	7.4%
Wetlands	5.0%

[...]

Effects on Climate Processes

Land use and land cover play critical roles in the interaction between the land and the atmosphere, influencing climate at local, regional, and global scales. There is growing evidence that land use, land cover, and land management affect the US climate in several ways:

- Air temperature and near-surface moisture are changed in areas where natural vegetation is converted to agriculture. This effect has been observed in the Great Plains and the Midwest, where overall dew point temperatures or the frequency of occurrences of extreme dew point temperatures have increased due to converting land to agricultural use. This effect has also been observed where the fringes of California's Central Valley are being converted from natural vegetation to agriculture. Other areas where uncultivated and conservation lands are being returned to cultivation, for example from restored grassland into biofuel production, have also experienced temperature shifts. Regional daily maximum temperatures were lowered due to forest clearing for agriculture in the Northeast and Midwest, and then increased in the Northeast following regrowth of forests due to abandonment of agriculture.
- Conversion of rain-fed cropland to irrigated agriculture further intensifies the impacts of agricultural conversion on temperature. For example, irrigation in California has been found to reduce daily maximum temperatures by up to 9°F. Model comparisons suggest that irrigation cools temperatures directly over croplands in California's Central Valley by 5°F to 13°F and increases relative humidity by 9% to 20%. Observational data-based studies found similar impacts of irrigated agriculture in the Great Plains.
- Both observational and modeling studies show that introduction of irrigated agriculture can alter regional precipitation. It has been shown that irrigation in the Ogallala aquifer portion of the Great Plains can affect precipitation as far away as Indiana and western Kentucky.
- Urbanization is having significant local impacts on weather and climate. Land-cover changes associated with urbanization are creating higher air temperatures compared to the

surrounding rural area. This is known as the "urban heat island" effect. Urban landscapes are also affecting formation of convective storms and changing the location and amounts of precipitation compared to pre-urbanization.

- Land-use and land-cover changes are affecting global atmospheric concentrations of greenhouse gases. The impact is expected to be most significant in areas with forest loss or gain, where the amount of carbon that can be transferred from the atmosphere to the land (or from the land to the atmosphere) is modified. Even in relatively un-forested areas, this effect can be significant. A recent USGS report suggests that from 2001 to 2005 in the Great Plains between 22 to 106 million metric tons of carbon were stored in the biosphere due to changes in land use and climate. Even with these seemingly large numbers, US forests absorb only 7% to 24% (with a best estimate of 16%) of fossil fuel CO_2 emissions.

Adapting to Climate Change

Land-use and land-cover patterns may be modified to adapt to anticipated or observed effects of a changed climate. These changes may be either encouraged or mandated by government (whether at federal or other levels), or undertaken by private initiative. In the US, even though land-use decisions are highly decentralized and strongly influenced by Constitutional protection of private property, the Supreme Court has also defined a role for government input into some land-use decisions. Thus on the one hand farmers may make private decisions to plant different crops in response to changing growing conditions and/or market prices. On the other hand, homeowners may be compelled to respond to policies, zoning, or regulations (at national, state, county, or municipal levels) by elevating their houses to reduce flood impacts associated with more intense rainfall events and/or increased impervious surfaces.

Land-use and land-cover changes are thus rarely the product of a single factor. Land-use decision processes are influenced not only by the biophysical environment, but also by markets, laws, technology, politics, perceptions, and culture. Yet there is evidence that climate adaptation considerations are playing an increasingly large role in land decisions, even in the absence of a formal federal climate policy. Motivations typically include avoiding or reducing negative impacts from extreme weather events (such as storms or heat waves) or from slow-onset hazards (such as sea level rise).

For example, New Orleans has, through a collection of private and public initiatives, rebuilt some of the neighborhoods damaged by Hurricane Katrina with housing elevated six feet or even higher above the ground and with roofs specially designed to facilitate evacuation. San Francisco has produced a land-use plan to reduce impacts from a rising San Francisco Bay. A similar concern has prompted collective action in four Miami-area counties and an array of San Diego jurisdictions, to name just two locales, to shape future land uses to comply with regulations linked to sea level rise projections. Chicago has produced a plan for limiting the number of casualties, especially among the elderly and homeless, during heat waves.

Reducing Greenhouse Gas Levels

Choices about land use and land management affect the amount of greenhouse gases entering and leaving the atmosphere and, therefore, provide opportunities to reduce climate change. Such choices can affect the balance of these gases directly, through decisions to preserve or restore carbon in standing vegetation (like forests) and soils, and indirectly, in the form of land-use policies that affect fossil fuel emissions by influencing energy consumption for transportation and in buildings. Additionally, as crops are increasingly used to make fuel, the potential for reducing net carbon emissions through replacement of fossil fuels represents a possible land-based carbon emissions reduction strategy, albeit one that is complicated by many natural and economic interactions that will determine the ultimate effect of these strategies on emissions.

Land-cover change and management accounts for about one-third of all carbon released into the atmosphere by people globally since 1850. The primary source related to land use has been the conversion of native vegetation like forests and grasslands to croplands, which in turn has released carbon from vegetation and soil into the atmosphere as carbon dioxide (CO_2). Currently, an estimated 16% of CO_2 going into the atmosphere is due to land-related activities globally, with the remainder coming from fossil fuel burning and cement manufacturing. In the United States, activities related to land use are effectively balanced with respect to CO_2: as much CO_2 is released to the atmosphere by land-use activities as is taken up by and stored in, for example, vegetation and soil. The regrowth of forests and increases of conservation-related forest and crop management practices have also increased carbon storage. Overall, setting aside emissions due to burning fossil fuels, in the US and the rest of North America, land cover takes up more carbon than it releases. This has happened as a result of more efficient forest and agricultural management practices, but it is not clear if this rate of uptake can be increased or if it will persist into the future. The projected declines in forest area put these carbon stores at risk. Additionally, the rate of carbon uptake on a given acre of forest can vary with weather, making it potentially sensitive to climate changes.

Opportunities to increase the net uptake of carbon from the atmosphere by the land include increasing the amount of area in ecosystems with high carbon content (by converting farms to forests or grasslands); increasing the rate of carbon uptake in existing ecosystems (through fertilization); and reducing carbon loss from existing ecosystems (for example, through no-till farming). Because of these effects, policies specifically aimed at increasing carbon storage, either directly through mandates or indirectly through a market for carbon offsets, may be used to encourage more land-based carbon storage.

The following uncertainties deserve further investigation: 1) the effects of these policies or actions on the balance of other greenhouse gases, like methane and nitrous oxide; 2) the degree of permanence these carbon stores will have in a changing climate (especially through the effects of disturbances like fires and plant pests); 3) the degree to which increases in carbon storage can be attributed to any specific policy, or whether or not they may have occurred without any policy change; and 4) the possibility that increased carbon storage in one location might be partially offset by releases in another. All of these specific mitigation options present implementation challenges, as the decisions must be weighed against competing objectives. For example, retiring farmland to sequester carbon may be difficult to achieve if crop prices rise, such as has occurred in recent years in response to the fast-growing market for biofuels. Agricultural research and development that increases the productivity of the sector presents the possibility of reducing demand for agricultural land and may serve as a powerful greenhouse gas mitigation strategy, although the ultimate net effect on greenhouse gas emissions is uncertain.

Land-use decisions in urban areas also present carbon reduction options. Carbon storage in urban areas can reach densities as high as those found in tropical forests, with most of that carbon found in soils, but also in vegetation, landfills, and the structures and contents of buildings. Urban and suburban areas tend to be net sources of carbon to the atmosphere, whereas exurban and rural areas tend to be net sinks. Effects of urban development patterns on carbon storage and emissions due to land and fossil fuel use are topics of current research and can be affected by land-use planning choices. Many cities have adopted land-use plans with explicit carbon goals, typically targeted at reducing carbon emissions from the often intertwined activities of transportation and energy use. This trend, which includes major cities such as Los Angeles, Chicago, and New York City as well as small towns, such as Homer, Alaska, has occurred even in the absence of a formal federal climate policy.

> "At many sites, the key reclamation, soil treatment, and water quality concerns owe their origin to the same process—the oxidation of sulfide minerals, especially the iron sulfide, pyrite. Oxidation of sulfide minerals can produce acidic conditions that release metals in both waste materials and water."

Mining's Impacts on the Environment Have Been Damaging

American Geosciences Institute

In the following viewpoint, the American Geosciences Institute argues that historically, the process of mining, while important to national economies, has had damaging effects on the environment. Older historic mines might continue to cause damage. But for new sites, there are ways to mitigate the costs to the environment. The authors note that these are reclamation, soil treatment, water treatment, preventing acid rock drainage, and controlling gas emissions. The American Geosciences Institute is an online resource that uses, summarizes, and links to information and documents from expert, nonpartisan, publicly available sources.

As you read, consider the following questions:

1. What is one of the challenges in using the reclamation approach, according to the viewpoint?
2. What is the active treatment process for treating acidic waters, according to the viewpoint?
3. What is one way acid rock drainage can be reduced?

The major potential environmental impacts associated with mining and associated mineral processing operations are related to erosion-prone landscapes, soil and water quality, and air quality. These potential impacts are recognized and addressed in current mining operations as well as in some former mining operations by reclaiming areas of physical disturbance to prevent erosion, stabilizing soils containing metals or chemicals to prevent unwanted metal releases into the environment, preventing and/or treating water contamination, and controlling air emissions.

Mitigating Impacts

At many sites, the key reclamation, soil treatment, and water quality concerns owe their origin to the same process—the oxidation of sulfide minerals, especially the iron sulfide, pyrite. Oxidation of sulfide minerals can produce acidic conditions that release metals in both waste materials and water.

Mining in the early days took place at a time when environmental impacts were not as well understood and, most importantly, not a matter of significant concern. As a result, historical mine sites may still have areas that are not reclaimed, remnants of facilities, and untreated water. This inherited legacy of environmental damage from mining is not indicative of the mining cycle today.

Now, mine closure and a number of activities to mitigate the impacts of mining are an integral part of all metal mine planning and mineral development from the discovery phase through to closure:

- Reclamation
- Soil treatment
- Water treatment
- Preventing acid rock drainage
- Controlling gas emissions

Reclamation

Reclamation entails the re-establishing of viable soils and vegetation at a mine site. Although regulatory agencies may require complex reclamation designs, simple approaches can be very effective. One simple approach depends on adding lime or other materials that will neutralize acidity plus a cover of top soil or suitable growth medium to promote vegetation growth. Modifying slopes and other surfaces and planting vegetation as part of the process stabilizes the soil material and prevents erosion and surface water infiltration. Even this simple approach is likely to cost a few thousand dollars per acre to implement. Where soils have a sustained high acidity, the costs of using this approach can increase, sometimes to tens of thousands of dollars per acre. The challenge to find cost-effective reclamation approaches continues.

Promising reclamation options in the future may include using sludge, "biosolids," from municipal waste water treatment processes as an organic soil amendment, and growing plant species that are more tolerant of acidic conditions.

Soil Treatment

High levels of metals in soils, not just acidity, can be harmful to plants, animals, and, in some cases, people. A common approach used in dealing with contaminated soil is to move it to specially designed repositories. This approach can be very expensive and controversial, but it is sometimes required. With this approach, the volume and toxicity of the soil is not reduced, the soil is just relocated. Effective soil treatment approaches in the future depend upon better understanding of the risks associated with metals in mine wastes. These "natural" metals in minerals may not be as readily available in the biosphere, and therefore, they may not be as toxic as the metals in processed forms, such as lead in gasoline.

Future approaches may include:

- Using chemical methods to stabilize metals in soils, making them less mobile and biologically available.
- Using bacteriacides that stop the bacterial growth that promotes the oxidation of pyrite and the accompanying formation of sulfuric acid.
- Using bioliners, such as low permeability and compacted manure, as barriers at the base of waste piles.
- Permanently flooding waste materials containing pyrite to cut off the source of oxygen, stop the development of acidic conditions, and prevent mobilization of metals.

Water Treatment

The most common treatment for acidic and metal-bearing waters is the addition of a neutralizing material, such as lime, to reduce the acidity. This "active" treatment process, which causes the dissolved metals to precipitate from the water, usually requires the construction of a treatment facility. The ongoing maintenance that such a plant requires makes this treatment technique very expensive.

Aside from the expense, some active treatment plants generate large amounts of sludge. Disposal of the sludge is a major problem. Because of the cost and the physical challenges of dealing with sludge, alternatives to active treatment facilities are needed. Some possible alternatives include:

- Using "passive" wetland systems to treat metal-bearing water. This approach has been successfully used where the volumes and acidity of the water are not too great. Passive wetland systems have the added advantage of creating desirable wildlife habitat.

Environmental Impacts of Urban Growth

We explore and quantify the manifold impacts of urbanization on ecosystems and the services they provide.

In determining the effects of urbanization on the environment we draw data from weather stations, field interviews, satellite images, and governmental records. We develop new algorithms for processing this data, apply spatial statistical analysis to discover trends, and use coupled human-environment system models to predict future impacts.

The conversion of Earth's land surface to urban uses is one of the most irreversible human impacts on the global biosphere. It hastens the loss of highly productive farmland, affects energy demand, alters the climate, modifies hydrologic and biogeochemical cycles, fragments habitats, and reduces biodiversity (Seto et al., 2011) We see these effects on multiple levels. Future urbanization will, for example, pose direct threats to high-value ecosystems: the highest rates of land conversion over the next few decades will likely take place in biodiversity hotspots that were relatively undisturbed by urban development in 2000 (Seto et al., 2012). Within cities, the nature of urban growth is also an important determinant of urban dwellers' vulnerability to environmental stress (Güneralp and Seto, 2008).

The environmental impacts of urban expansion reach far beyond urban areas themselves. In rapidly urbanizing areas, agriculture intensifies on remaining undeveloped land and is likely to expand to new areas, putting pressure on land resources (Jiang et al., 2013). Furthermore, urban areas change precipitation patterns at scales of hundreds of square kilometers (Kaufman et al., 2007). Urban expansion will affect global climate as well. Direct loss in vegetation biomass from areas with high probability of urban expansion is predicted to contribute about 5% of total emissions from tropical deforestation and land-use change (Seto et al., 2012). The scope and scale of these impacts is yet to be fully researched. Although many studies have described how urbanization affects CO_2 emissions and heat budgets, effects on the circulation of water, aerosols, and nitrogen in the climate system are only beginning to be understood (Seto & Shepherd, 2009).

"Environmental Impacts of Urban Growth," Yale University.

- Using in-situ treatment zones where reactive materials or electric currents are placed in the subsurface so that water passing through them would be treated.
- Combining treatment with the recovery of useful materials from contaminated water.

Preventing Acid Rock Drainage

Although the discharge of acidic drainage presents several challenges to protecting water quality, the significance and widespread occurrence of acid rock drainage warrant special efforts to prevent or minimize its occurrence. Prevention must be addressed during exploration activities, before the beginning of newly-planned mining operations. In some cases, it may even be possible to prevent or reduce acid rock drainage in old or abandoned mining areas. Current and potential treatment approaches for acid rock drainage are similar to those already described. Possible measures to prevent or significantly reduce acid rock drainage include:

- Flooding of old underground mine workings to cut off the oxygen supply necessary to the sustained generation of acidic waters.
- Sealing exposed surfaces in underground workings with a coating of material that is non-reactive or impermeable to inhibit the oxidation process.
- Backfilling mine workings with reactive materials that can neutralize and treat waters that pass through them.
- Adding chemicals to the water in flooded surface and underground mine workings that can inhibit acid-generating chemical reactions and precipitate coatings that will seal off groundwater migration routes.
- Isolating contaminated waters at depth by stratification, allowing viable habitat to develop near the surface in the water that fills large open pits.

Controlling Smelter Emissions

Smelter emissions, especially sulfur dioxide and particulate materials, have historically presented significant environmental problems. Modern smelting technology has met this challenge by drastically reducing the amount of emissions. An example is the modernized smelter built by Kennecott Utah Copper that processes ore concentrates from the Bingham Canyon Mine near Salt Lake City. Using technology developed by the Finnish company Outokumpu, this smelter has reduced sulfur dioxide emissions to 95 percent of previous permitted levels. This smelter, which came online in 1995, is the cleanest in the world. It captures 99.9 percent of the emitted sulfur.

> *"Reaching toward the goal of sustainable agriculture is the responsibility of all participants in the system, including farmers, laborers, policymakers, researchers, retailers, and consumers."*

Sustainable Agriculture Can Meet Society's Needs Today Without Compromising Society's Needs of the Future

Gail Feenstra, Chuck Ingels, and David Campbell

In the following excerpted viewpoint, Gail Feenstra, Chuck Ingels, and David Campbell argue that sustainable farming has a very real goal that can be achieved if everyone in the food system plays a part. The authors note that following these practices also requires a commitment to changing public policies, economic institutions, and social values. Land use planners and decision makers should be educated about sustainable agriculture, as well. Feenstra is deputy director of the UC ANR Sustainable Agriculture Research and Education Program, a program of the Agricultural Sustainability Institute at the University of California, Davis. Ingels was perennial cropping systems analyst at the program. Campbell is the program's former economic and public policy analyst.

As you read, consider the following questions:

1. What are sustainable agriculture's three main goals, as outlined in the viewpoint?
2. What reason do the authors give for the decline of ancient civilizations such as Mesopotamia?
3. What is the conundrum of agriculture's reliance on nonrenewable energy sources?

A griculture has changed dramatically, especially since the end of World War II. Food and fiber productivity soared due to new technologies, mechanization, increased chemical use, specialization and government policies that favored maximizing production. These changes allowed fewer farmers with reduced labor demands to produce the majority of the food and fiber in the US.

Although these changes have had many positive effects and reduced many risks in farming, there have also been significant costs. Prominent among these are topsoil depletion, groundwater contamination, the decline of family farms, continued neglect of the living and working conditions for farm laborers, increasing costs of production, and the disintegration of economic and social conditions in rural communities.

A growing movement has emerged during the past two decades to question the role of the agricultural establishment in promoting practices that contribute to these social problems. Today this movement for sustainable agriculture is garnering increasing support and acceptance within mainstream agriculture. Not only does sustainable agriculture address many environmental and social concerns, but it offers innovative and economically viable opportunities for growers, laborers, consumers, policymakers and many others in the entire food system.

This page is an effort to identify the ideas, practices and policies that constitute our concept of sustainable agriculture. We do so for two reasons: 1) to clarify the research agenda and priorities of our program, and 2) to suggest to others practical steps that may be appropriate for them in moving toward sustainable agriculture. Because the concept of sustainable agriculture is still evolving, we intend this page not as a definitive or final statement, but as an invitation to continue the dialogue.

What Is Sustainable Agriculture?

Sustainable agriculture integrates three main goals—environmental health, economic profitability, and social and economic equity. A variety of philosophies, policies and practices have contributed to these goals. People in many different capacities, from farmers to consumers, have shared this vision and contributed to it. Despite the diversity of people and perspectives, the following themes commonly weave through definitions of sustainable agriculture:

Sustainability rests on the principle that we must meet the needs of the present without compromising the ability of future generations to meet their own needs. Therefore, stewardship of both natural and human resources is of prime importance. Stewardship of human resources includes consideration of social responsibilities such as working and living conditions of laborers, the needs of rural communities, and consumer health and safety both in the present and the future. Stewardship of land and natural resources involves maintaining or enhancing this vital resource base for the long term.

A systems perspective is essential to understanding sustainability. The system is envisioned in its broadest sense, from the individual farm, to the local ecosystem, and to communities affected by this farming system both locally and globally. An emphasis on the system allows a larger and more thorough view of the consequences of farming practices on both human communities and the environment. A systems approach gives us the tools to explore the interconnections between farming and other aspects of our environment.

A systems approach also implies interdisciplinary efforts in research and education. This requires not only the input of researchers from various disciplines, but also farmers, farmworkers, consumers, policymakers and others.

Making the transition to sustainable agriculture is a process. For farmers, the transition to sustainable agriculture normally requires a series of small, realistic steps. Family economics and personal goals influence how fast or how far participants can go in the transition. It is important to realize that each small decision can make a difference and contribute to advancing the entire system further on the "sustainable agriculture continuum." The key to moving forward is the will to take the next step.

Finally, it is important to point out that reaching toward the goal of sustainable agriculture is the responsibility of all participants in the system, including farmers, laborers, policymakers, researchers, retailers, and consumers. Each group has its own part to play, its own unique contribution to make to strengthen the sustainable agriculture community.

Farming and Natural Resources

When the production of food and fiber degrades the natural resource base, the ability of future generations to produce and flourish decreases. The decline of ancient civilizations in Mesopotamia, the Mediterranean region, Pre-Columbian southwest US and Central America is believed to have been strongly influenced by natural resource degradation from non-sustainable farming and forestry practices.

Groundwater Contamination

Water is the principal resource that has helped agriculture and society to prosper, and it has been a major limiting factor when mismanaged.

In California, an extensive water storage and transfer system has been established which has allowed crop production to expand to very arid regions. In drought years, limited surface water supplies have prompted overdraft of groundwater and consequent intrusion of salt water, or permanent collapse of aquifers. Periodic droughts, some lasting up to 50 years, have occurred in California.

Several steps should be taken to develop drought-resistant farming systems even in "normal" years, including both policy and management actions:

1) improving water conservation and storage measures,
2) providing incentives for selection of drought-tolerant crop species,
3) using reduced-volume irrigation systems,
4) managing crops to reduce water loss, or
5) not planting at all.

The most important issues related to water quality involve salinization and contamination of ground and surface waters by pesticides, nitrates and selenium. Salinity has become a problem wherever water of even relatively low salt content is used on shallow soils in arid regions and/or where the water table is near the root zone of crops. Tile drainage can remove the water and salts, but the disposal of the salts and other contaminants may negatively affect the environment depending upon where they are deposited. Temporary solutions include the use of salt-tolerant crops, low-volume irrigation, and various management techniques to minimize the effects of salts on crops. In the long-term, some farmland may need to be removed from production or converted to other uses. Other uses include conversion of row crop land to production of drought-tolerant forages, the restoration of wildlife habitat or the use of agroforestry to minimize the impacts of salinity and high water tables.

Another way in which agriculture affects water resources is through the destruction of riparian habitats within watersheds. The conversion of wild habitat to agricultural land reduces fish and wildlife through erosion and sedimentation, the effects of pesticides, removal of riparian plants, and the diversion of water. The plant diversity in and around both riparian and agricultural areas should be maintained in order to support a diversity of wildlife. This diversity will enhance natural ecosystems and could aid in agricultural pest management.

Energy

Modern agriculture is heavily dependent on non-renewable energy sources, especially petroleum. The continued use of these energy sources cannot be sustained indefinitely, yet to abruptly abandon our reliance on them would be economically catastrophic. However, a sudden cutoff in energy supply would be equally disruptive. In sustainable agricultural systems, there is reduced reliance on non-renewable energy sources and a substitution of renewable sources or labor to the extent that is economically feasible.

Air

Many agricultural activities affect air quality. These include smoke from agricultural burning; dust from tillage, traffic and harvest; pesticide drift from spraying; and nitrous oxide emissions from the use of nitrogen fertilizer. Options to improve air quality include:

- incorporating crop residue into the soil
- using appropriate levels of tillage
- and planting wind breaks, cover crops or strips of native perennial grasses to reduce dust.

Soil

Soil erosion continues to be a serious threat to our continued ability to produce adequate food. Numerous practices have been developed to keep soil in place, which include:

- reducing or eliminating tillage
- managing irrigation to reduce runoff
- and keeping the soil covered with plants or mulch.

[…]

The Economic, Social & Political Context

In addition to strategies for preserving natural resources and changing production practices, sustainable agriculture requires a commitment to changing public policies, economic institutions, and social values. Strategies for change must take into account the complex, reciprocal and ever-changing relationship between agricultural production and the broader society.

The "food system" extends far beyond the farm and involves the interaction of individuals and institutions with contrasting and often competing goals including farmers, researchers, input suppliers, farmworkers, unions, farm advisors, processors, retailers, consumers, and policymakers. Relationships among these actors shift over time as new technologies spawn economic, social and political changes.

A wide diversity of strategies and approaches are necessary to create a more sustainable food system. These will range from specific and concentrated efforts to alter specific policies or practices, to the longer-term tasks of reforming key institutions, rethinking economic priorities, and challenging widely-held social values. Areas of concern where change is most needed include the following:

Food and Agricultural Policy

Existing federal, state and local government policies often impede the goals of sustainable agriculture. New policies are needed to simultaneously promote environmental health, economic profitability, and social and economic equity. For example, commodity and price support programs could be restructured to allow farmers to realize the full benefits of the productivity gains made possible through alternative practices. Tax and credit policies could be modified to encourage a diverse and decentralized system of family farms rather than corporate concentration and absentee ownership. Government and land grant university research policies could be modified to emphasize the development of sustainable alternatives. Marketing orders and cosmetic standards could be amended to encourage reduced pesticide use. Coalitions must be created to address these policy concerns at the local, regional, and national level.

Land Use

Conversion of agricultural land to urban uses is a particular concern in California, as rapid growth and escalating land values threaten farming on prime soils. Existing farmland conversion patterns often discourage farmers from adopting sustainable practices and a long-term perspective on the value of land. At the same time, the close proximity of newly developed residential areas to farms is increasing the public demand for environmentally safe farming practices. Comprehensive new policies to protect prime soils and regulate development are needed, particularly in California's Central Valley. By helping farmers to adopt practices that reduce chemical use and conserve scarce resources, sustainable agriculture research and education can play a key role in building public support for agricultural land preservation. Educating land use planners and decision-makers about sustainable agriculture is an important priority.

Labor

In California, the conditions of agricultural labor are generally far below accepted social standards and legal protections in other forms of employment. Policies and programs are needed to address this problem, working toward socially just and safe employment that provides adequate wages, working conditions, health benefits, and chances for economic stability. The needs of migrant labor for year-around employment and adequate housing are a particularly crucial problem needing immediate attention. To be more sustainable over the long-term, labor must be acknowledged and supported by government policies, recognized as important constituents of land grant universities, and carefully considered when assessing the impacts of new technologies and practices.

Rural Community Development

Rural communities in California are currently characterized by economic and environmental deterioration. Many are among the poorest locations in the nation. The reasons for the decline are complex, but changes in farm structure have played a significant role. Sustainable agriculture presents an opportunity to rethink the importance of family farms and rural communities. Economic development policies are needed that encourage more diversified agricultural production on family farms as a foundation for healthy economies in rural communities. In combination with other strategies, sustainable agriculture practices and policies can help foster community institutions that meet employment, educational, health, cultural and spiritual needs.

Consumers and the Food System

Consumers can play a critical role in creating a sustainable food system. Through their purchases, they send strong messages to producers, retailers and others in the system about what they think is important. Food cost and nutritional quality have always influenced consumer choices. The challenge now is to find strategies that broaden consumer perspectives, so that environmental quality, resource use, and social equity issues are also considered in shopping decisions. At the same time, new policies and institutions must be created to enable producers using sustainable practices to market their goods to a wider public. Coalitions organized around improving the food system are one specific method of creating a dialogue among consumers, retailers, producers and others. These coalitions or other public forums can be important vehicles for clarifying issues, suggesting new policies, increasing mutual trust, and encouraging a long-term view of food production, distribution and consumption.

> *"When you erode these wildernesses,
> they don't come back, you can't
> restore them. They will come back
> as something else, but you can't
> restore them."*

Humans Have Destroyed a Tenth of Earth's Wilderness in Twenty-Five Years

Adam Vaughan

In the following viewpoint, Adam Vaughan argues that human activity has caused the destruction of a large percentage of the planet's wilderness. The depletion of wilderness is associated with many negative results, such as higher carbon emissions, extinction of native species, and pollution. Experts are focusing on what remains, imploring governments to enact policies that will protect places such as the Amazon rain forest. Once these environments are gone, the author notes, they are difficult or impossible to restore. Vaughan is energy correspondent for the Guardian.

"Humans Have Destroyed a Tenth of Earth's Wilderness in 25 Years—Study," by Adam Vaughan, Guardian News and Media Limited, September 8, 2016. Reprinted by permission.

As you read, consider the following questions:

1. What area of the world accounted for nearly a third of catastrophic loss of wilderness?
2. Why do the remaining wildernesses need to be protected, according to the expert quoted in the viewpoint?
3. What percentage of the planet's land area is still wildnerness, according to the viewpoint?

Humans have destroyed a tenth of Earth's remaining wilderness in the last 25 years and there may be none left within a century if trends continue, according to an authoritative new study.

Researchers found a vast area the size of two Alaskas—3.3m square kilometres—had been tarnished by human activities between 1993 and today, which experts said was a "shockingly bad" and "profoundly large number."

The Amazon accounted for nearly a third of the "catastrophic" loss, showing huge tracts of pristine rainforest are still being disrupted despite the Brazilian government slowing deforestation rates in recent years. A further 14% disappeared in central Africa, home to thousands of species including forest elephants and chimpanzees.

The loss of the world's last untouched refuges would not just be disastrous for endangered species but for climate change efforts, the authors said, because some of the forests store enormous amounts of carbon.

"Without any policies to protect these areas, they are falling victim to widespread development. We probably have one to two decades to turn this around," said lead author Dr James Watson, of the University of Queensland and Wildlife Conservation Society.

The analysis defined wilderness as places that are "ecologically largely intact" and "mostly free of human disturbance," though

THE POSITIVE IMPACTS OF LAND USE CHANGE

In the face of growing land use change, resource scarcity, and degradation we recognize dominant negative attributions. However, there is also reason to believe that anthropogenic land use change can have positive effects on both, human well-being and sustainable ecosystem developments. For instance, traditional land use in temperate regions has led to an increase in biodiversity with its associated functions.

Firstly, we identify temporal and spatial exemplifications of positive land use changes. For instance, in "young domesticated" landscapes—with close-to-nature ecosystems—human interventions have a negative impact on biodiversity (fragmentation). In "old" cultivated landscapes, on the other hand, the preservation of biodiversity is linked with the preservation of land use diversity (and old usages). We reflect the idea that there are positive aspects of land use change over space and time.

Secondly, solutions for sustainable land use are usually discussed in an either-or manner, e.g. land sharing vs. land sparing. Preferably a diplomatic solution is presented representing the optimum between all tradeoffs multiple disciplines are aware of. Our considerations

some have indigenous people living within them. The team counted areas as no longer wilderness if they scored on eight measures of humanity's footprint, including roads, lights at night and agriculture.

The largest chunk of wilderness in the Amazon basin shrank from 1.8m sq km to 1.3m sq km, while the Ucayali moist forests in the west of the Amazon, home to more than 600 bird species and primates including emperor tamarins, was badly affected. The trajectory of loss in the world's biggest rainforest was "particularly concerning," the authors warned, given it happened despite deforestation rates slowing.

In Africa, none of the lowland forest in the western Congo basin is now considered globally significant wilderness, the study reach out to the hypothesis that one optimal solution would lead to a less diverse globe. Counterintuitive we argue that a diversity of land use options including extremes derived from a monodisciplinary aspect are needed to preserve both biodiversity and cultural diversity. Overall the best mix of solutions has to be regionally tailored under consideration of national and global pattern. That means, solutions can range from small scale diverse land systems to large scale mono-structural land system. Therefore we propose to develop a catalog of single disciplinary solutions based on context, scale and time preferences.

Thirdly, combining insights from different disciplinary perspectives, we hold that positive motivation leads to an optimization of land use. Biodiversity, as well as cultural diversity, are mainly considered as goods of common interest inheriting high values that need to be protected. Interaction between the both, however, are perceived among the fundamental clashes between man and nature and peaks in land use. Therefore, the focus should be on positive aspects: different landscapes fulfill different ecosystem services and contribute to different SDGs. Through supra-regional agreements, it can be ensured that all functions of ecosystems are sustained (or improved).

"Positive Impacts Through Land Use Change," DKNsummit18.org, German Committee Future Earth.

found. WWF believes the area is possibly home to more gorillas and chimpanzees than other area in the world.

The study said that wilderness was being lost faster than pristine places were being designated as protected areas, at 3.3m sq km versus 2.5m sq km.

Professor William Laurance of James Cook University said: "Environmental policies are failing the world's vanishing wildernesses. Despite being strongholds for imperilled biodiversity, regulating local climates, and sustaining many indigenous communities, wilderness areas are vanishing before our eye."

The study said the reason was that such areas are "assumed to be relatively free from threatening processes and therefore are not a priority for conservation efforts."

The ramifications of remaining wilderness being corrupted were wide-ranging and irreversible for both people and wildlife, Watson said.

"There are four reasons why we need to protect these places. One is biodiversity, the second is carbon, the third is the poorest of the poor are living in them, and the fourth is this is a reference point for nature, of pre-human environments," he told the *Guardian*.

The Earth's remaining wilderness areas are strongholds for many of the land-based mammals on the red list of endangered species, which was updated this week to reveal that four of the world's six great apes are now critically endangered.

Losing forests in these areas could also affect leaders' efforts to rein in greenhouse gas emissions to tackle climate change, the study said, because of the amount of carbon stored in trees and peat.

Rewilding plans by conservationists, similar to efforts to reintroduce wolves, lynx and other species to the UK, could also be harmed by the loss of wilderness, because the world risked losing a true picture of what certain ecosystems looked like.

"Without concerted preservation of existing wilderness areas, there will be a diminished capacity for large-scale ecological restoration," the authors wrote.

Watson said unique ecosystems were being lost, and there was no turning back. "What is critical about this paper is when you erode these wildernesses, they don't come back, you can't restore them. They will come back as something else, but you can't restore them," he said.

The study, published in the journal *Current Biology* on Thursday, predicted that if current trends continue there could be no globally significantly wild areas left in "less than a century."

However, the mapping exercise found that there is still 30m sq km of wilderness globally, 23% of the world's land area. Strongholds include the boreal forests of northern Canada, Australia's deserts and western woodlands, some lowland forests in Asia and parts of central Africa.

"They are the jewels in the crown. We have obligation to protect them in same way as we do species," said Watson.

Stopping or slowing the loss of wilderness will require governments to put in place national strategies that recognise their value, the authors said. One Brazilian programme that supported the creation of protected areas to save carbon and help indigenous people was singled out as the type of project that could help address the decline.

But the authors admitted that: "[such] positive examples are too few, and we argue that immediate action to protect the world's remaining wilderness areas on a large scale is now necessary, including in global policy platforms."

Carlos Rittl, executive secretary of the Brazilian Climate Observatory, said: "This paper is a powerful reminder of the key role forests play on climate targets, and should be taken at heart by policymakers. Despite the recent drop in deforestation rates, Brazil is still the tropical country that most loses forests every year.

"Our Paris pledge on deforestation is shamefully weak—we are comformed with ending only illegal deforestation only by 2030 and only in Amazonia—and we don't even have a plan for achieving that little. Brazil will ratify the Paris agreement next Monday. If the government is serious about meeting the deal's long-term goal, it should be talking about zero deforestation."

Mike Barrett, WWF-UK's director of science and policy, said: "This vast scale of loss in global wilderness is having grave impacts. As we seemingly enter the Anthropocene era, this report further signifies humanity's immense impact and the effects that is having for wildlife and people alike."

He pointed to the recent red list update which showed the situation of giant pandas improving, but said: "While flagship species and habitats have an important role in tackling the biodiversity crisis, this alone won't solve the problem. We need significant changes in how we value our planet as at present we're taking relentlessly from our oceans, rivers, forests and wilderness."

The study comes as the world's top conservationists conclude their meeting in Hawaii this week on dozens of motions for protecting wildlife, including restrictions on the trade in the pangolin, the world's most trafficked animal, and calls on governments to keep harmful activity such as oil drilling out of protected areas.

Later this month governments are due to attend a major meeting in Johannesburg to discuss the legal trade in endangered species, including the fate of the current international ban on the trade in ivory.

Periodical and Internet Sources Bibliography

The following articles have been selected to supplement the diverse views presented in this chapter.

Vanessa M. Adams, Robert L. Pressey, and Jorge G. Alvarez-Romero, "Using Optimal Land-Use Scenarios to Assess Trade-Offs Between Conservation, Development, and Social Values," *PLOS One*, June 30, 2016. https://www.ncbi.nlm.nih.gov/pmc/articles /PMC4928809.

Hans Bader, "NYT: Biofuel Mandates Have Been an Environmental Disaster," Foundation for Economic Education, November 27, 2018. https://fee.org/articles/nyt-biofuel-mandates-have-been -an-environmental-disaster.

E.S.L., "Why Henry George Had a Point," *Economist*, April 2, 2015. https://www.economist.com/free-exchange/2015/04/01/why -henry-george-had-a-point.

David Cay Johnston, "The Hidden Costs of the World's Ghost Apartments," *Newsweek*, April 14, 2015. https://www.newsweek .com/2015/04/24/hidden-costs-ghost-apartments-322264.html.

Laura Latham, "Reclamation Mark," *Financial Times*, May 3, 2013. https://www.ft.com/content/41f154a4-acf2-11e2-b27f -00144feabdc0.

Andrew Meeker, "Land Use Planning and the Contest for the Meaning of Nature," Angles from the *Carolina Planning Journal*, June 4, 2018. https://carolinaangles.com/2018/06/04/land-use -planning-and-the-contest-for-the-meaning-of-nature.

Josy O'Donnel, "Land Pollution: Causes, Effects, and Solutions for the Future," Conservation Institute, May 15, 2018. https://www .conservationinstitute.org/land-pollution.

Matthew Turner, "The Economics of Land-Use Regulations," PERC, January 12, 2015. https://www.perc.org/2015/01/12/the -economics-of-land-use-regulations.

Alden Wicker, "Fast Fashion Is Creating an Environmental Crisis," *Newsweek*, September 1, 2016. https://www.newsweek.com /2016/09/09/old-clothes-fashion-waste-crisis-494824.html.

Chris Woodford, "Land Pollution," Explain That Stuff, March 27, 2018. https://www.explainthatstuff.com/land-pollution.html.

CHAPTER 4

Why Is It Important to Consider the Effects of Land Development and Use on the Environment?

Chapter Preface

Human activity has had an impact on the environment over time, in ways both big and small. Rising populations and increasing consumption threaten to deplete our natural resources, suggesting a poor future for the human race. It's the future that is the most troubling; that future should be the motivator to change practices that are harming the planet.

To meet the needs of a growing population, cities develop new neighborhoods, build new homes, and construct new commercial buildings. This is exciting and fruitful for many, but care must be taken to plan locations and design buildings and resource systems that do not disrupt the original ecosystem.

There may be a tendency to presume that any farmland is preferable to urban development or suburban sprawl. But agriculture can deplete the resources of the land if not managed correctly.

Land use regulation is a touchy subject. Critics argue that government oversight is unnecessary and costly. Supporters counter that regulation protects land, water quality, and wildlife, which ultimately helps the planet and human well-being. Civic and government policies that would please both sides can be enacted.

Some say fears about the planet's future are overblown. But the planet has a finite land and limited resources. Isn't it worth changing our ways to maintain them?

> *"A fundamental issue in previous technological revolutions has been the lightness with which we have taken for granted healthy natural systems like forests, oceans, river basins (all underpinned and maintained by biodiversity) rather than valuing these as a necessary condition to development."*

Technology Can Help Us Save the Planet

Marco Lambertini

In the following viewpoint, Marco Lambertini argues that technology can help decouple development and environmental degradation. The author notes that the planet is in trouble, with increasing rates of consumption each year resulting in depletion of species and ecosystems. In order to build a healthy and prosperous future on earth, the author suggests looking to developments that are the antithesis of the natural world, such as blockchain technology, drones, thermal imaging, and artificial intelligence. Lambertini is director-general at World Wildlife Fund (WWF).

"Technology Can Help Us Save the Planet. But More than Anything, We Must Learn to Value Nature," by Marco Lambertini, World Economic Forum, August 23, 2018. Reprinted by permission.

As you read, consider the following questions:

1. In how many months of 2018 did we consume a year's worth of resources, according to the viewpoint?
2. How has technology helped detect illegal logging?
3. How is artificial intelligence being used to protect wild tigers and their habitats?

Technology is fundamentally changing the way we live, work, relate to one another and to the external world. The speed, breadth and depth of current breakthroughs has no historical precedent and is disrupting almost every sector in every country. Now more than ever, the advent of new technology has the potential to transform environmental protection.

The hunt for new smarter ways to support our development has always been a key driver of technological advancement. Today as our civilisation faces a new unprecedented challenge, technology can play a crucial role in decoupling development and environmental degradation.

Let's be clear. No human technology can fully replace "nature's technology" perfected over hundreds of millions of years in delivering key services to sustain life on Earth. A productive, diverse natural world, and a stable climate have been the foundation of the success of our civilization, and will continue to be so in future. A fundamental issue in previous technological revolutions has been the lightness with which we have taken for granted healthy natural systems like forests, oceans, river basins (all underpinned and maintained by biodiversity) rather than valuing these as a necessary condition to development.

We Consume More Natural Resources than the Planet Can Regenerate

On 1 August, the world hit Earth Overshoot Day, the point in our calendars when we tip into consuming more natural resources than the planet can regenerate in a year.

Global Footprint Network, an international non-profit that calculates how we are managing—or failing to manage—the world's resources, says that in the first seven months of 2018 we devoured a year's worth of resources, such as water, to produce everything from the food on our plates to the clothes we're wearing—a new unwanted record.

At present, we are using resources and ecosystem services as though we had 1.7 Earths and such an ecological overshoot is possible only for a limited time before ecosystems begin to degrade and, ultimately, collapse.

As global biodiversity continues to decline steeply, the health and functioning of crucial ecosystems like forests, the ocean, rivers and wetlands will be affected. Coupled with climate change impacts which are evident in warnings from scientists and the increasing frequency and intensity of extreme weather events worldwide; this is going to be disastrous for the ecological balance of the planet and for our survival. Earth Overshoot Day is a stark reminder of the urgent actions individuals, countries and the global community must take to protect forests, oceans, wildlife and freshwater resources and help achieve resilience and sustainable development for all.

We have a critical window of opportunity between now and 2020 to put in place commitments and actions to reverse the trend of nature loss by 2030 and help ensure the health and well-being of people and our planet.

This Is Not Just Doom and Gloom, the Risk Is Real

The failing of natural systems is not without consequences for us.

Every day new evidence of our unsustainable impact on the environment is emerging. The last five years have been the warmest five-year period on record, the Arctic warmed much faster than predicted and the UN estimates that in the last 10 years, climate-related disasters have caused $1.4 trillion worth of damage worldwide.

In just over 40 years, the world has witnessed 60% decline in wildlife across land, sea and freshwater and is heading towards a shocking decline of two-thirds by 2020 if current trends continue. This has happened in less than a generation. A blink of the eye, compared to the hundreds of millions of years some of these species have lived on our planet.

Forests are under pressure like never before with unabated deforestation and at sea, 90% of the world's fish stocks are overfished. All indicators point toward our planet being on the brink.

Why does this matter? It matters because we will not build a stable, prosperous and equitable future on a depleted planet.

The "Battle of Technologies"

It is time to focus on the solutions which we know exist or have the potential to be developed and this is where technology, along with behavioural change, can help us reboot the health of our nature and planet.

From the high seas to the depths of the world's most dense forests, technology can transform how we identify, measure, track and value the many services and resources nature provides us with.

Blockchain to Revolutionize the Commodity Markets

Earlier this year, WWF in Australia, Fiji and New Zealand joined forces to stamp out illegal fishing and slave labour in the tuna fishing industry using blockchain technology. "From bait to plate," the advances in blockchain technology can help consumers track the entire journey of their tuna—and potentially other agricultural commodities and fish—revolutionizing systems of certification and traceability. We can also use satellite data and cost-effective GPS tracking devices to "see" and understand global fishing and global vessel traffic.

Remote Sensing in Planning and Monitoring

On land as well, remote sensing plays an important role in planning, monitoring, and evaluating impact on the ground. It has enabled WWF to monitor the developments of extractive

The Impact of Buildings on the Environment

Buildings are one of the enduring symbols of human society and the development process. They require a vast input of raw materials to build, operate, and maintain. As such, the contribution of buildings to societies' collective environmental footprint is sizable. In order to measure these impacts and encourage sustainable development, a slew of environmental assessment tools have been created. Among the many methods to quantify environmental impact is the life cycle assessment (LCA). LCA assesses production stages — from the raw materials to the finished product — and measures contribution to a wide array of environmental impacts, such as global warming, human toxicity, terrestrial eco-toxicity, and land use. It is meant to be comprehensive in order to prevent shifting environmental burdens from one impact category to another. But currently relatively few LCA studies of buildings and other products consider land use.

In order to assess the importance of this omission, authors from the European Union published a study in the International Journal of Life Cycle Assessment, examining the impacts of land use generated by both wood and cement construction of a standard single-family

industries in socially and ecologically-sensitive areas, including World Heritage sites.

We're also partnering with NASA's Jet Propulsion Lab (JPL) and UCLA to develop an algorithm that enables the detection of deforestation from palm oil expansion using remote sensing data, and we're exploring the potential to expand this technology to other commodities.

Drones and Crowdsourcing Help Monitor Forest Health and Detect Illegal Logging

Protecting the world's forests means ensuring land—in the right places—is protected or restored as well as healthy, providing people and wildlife what they need to survive, like clean air and water, home. They pose three main questions: Is land use a decisive factor in the environmental footprint of a building? How important is the building lot compared to land use in the supply-chain? And how do the different home constructions compare?

The study uncovers a number of key findings related to the assessment of land use impacts in building life cycle assessment. Most broadly, the study finds that the assignment of land use impacts can be a deciding factor in determining the cumulative impact of one structure versus another. This is due to the greater land use demands of timber and other biological building materials. Just as importantly the study finds that there is a need for greater agreement, or at least careful selection, among the different methods used to measure land use impacts. This is an area of active development within the LCA community, and the authors recommend that new methods being developed be quickly implemented within LCA software tools. This will allow their results to be tested while giving practitioners an enhanced ability to assess the importance of land use burdens in the overall environmental impact of the products, processes, and buildings that make the modern world go round.

"How important is land use to building environmental impact?" by Ben Morelli, Yale University, November 9, 2015.

food and jobs. And that's where drones come in to play, acting as our eyes on the forest. And it's not just WWF that is using this technology.

WRI (World Research Institute) has developed Global Forest Watch (GFW), an online forest monitoring and alert system that uses crowdsourcing, to allow anyone to create custom maps, analyse forest trends, subscribe to alerts, or download data for their local area or the entire world.

Thermal Imaging to Combat Poaching

Every night, park rangers patrol the pitch-black savanna of Kenya's Maasai Mara National Reserve. They search for armed poachers who spill across the border from Tanzania to hunt for bush meat and ivory. For years the number of poachers overwhelmed the relatively small cadre of rangers. Technology is now helping to turn the tide. Thermal imaging video cameras enable rangers to catch poachers at record rates and deter many more from even making the attempt.

Beyond direct interventions to stop poaching, WWF also uses technology to go after wildlife traffickers. To that end, we're working with a coalition of leading e-commerce and social media giants in the US and China to root out the sale of illicit wildlife products on their platforms.

AI to Track Wildlife

It is hard to think of technology and nature together but even advances like Artificial Intelligence (AI) that could not be further removed from the natural world are helping conservation efforts.

In China, WWF and tech giant Intel are harnessing the power of AI to help protect wild tigers and their habitats, while also protecting countless other species as a result while helping carbon storage, vital watersheds and communities in the area.

An Engaged Public Is Critical

As we engage new partners and pursue novel applications of technology, we believe an informed and engaged public is critical to this work and we are constantly looking to make people aware of the challenges facing our planet and what we're doing to solve them. In 2016, we partnered with Apple to create an Apps for Earth campaign that raised $8 million and educated millions of people around the world about core conservation issues. More recently, we leveraged Apple's augmented reality tools to launch the "WWF Free Rivers" app that invites people to experience the importance of free-flowing rivers for nature and for humans, and demonstrates how ill-conceived economic development endangers them both.

The possibilities for technology partnerships to reboot nature are endless. Our challenge now is to scale this work beyond a few test sites and into all of the places we are working to protect the planet. More than technology, we need a fundamental shift in mindset and understanding of the role that nature and biodiversity plays in our lives and businesses.

If we continue to produce, consume and power our lives the way we do right now, forests, oceans and weather systems will be overwhelmed and collapse. Unsustainable agriculture, fisheries, infrastructure projects, mining and energy are leading to unprecedented biodiversity loss and habitat degradation, over-exploitation, pollution and climate change.

While their impacts are increasingly evident in the natural world, the consequences on people are real too. From food and water scarcity to the quality of the air we breathe, the evidence has never been clearer. We are however, in many instances, failing to make the link. Alongside the technological revolution, what we need is an equally unprecedented cultural revolution in the way we connect with the planet.

> "Recent efforts to increase forest
> cover through reforestation and
> afforestation programs have helped
> to reduce deforestation but they do
> not fully restore lost biodiversity,
> which is built over hundreds of
> years and comprises complex and
> diverse biomes."

A Business as Usual Model for the Future Is Not Sustainable

United Nations

In the following excerpted viewpoint, the United Nations examines the likely scenario for a future in which nothing was changed regarding land use. Land use and land cover change (LUCC) is posing a grave danger to earth's ecosystems. The authors state that it is essential that the international community come together to agree on best practices for managing the preservation of ecosystems. The United Nations is a global organization that brings together its member states to protect human rights, maintain peace and security, deliver humanitarian aid, and uphold international law around the world.

From "Sustainable Land Use for the 21st Century," Sustainable Development Goals, ©2012 United Nations. Reprinted with the permission of the United Nations.

As you read, consider the following questions:

1. What percentage of the world's population experiences severe water scarcity, according to the viewpoint?
2. According to the authors, what is the ultimate benefit of land use?
3. What is one challenge in getting developing countries to implement payments for ecosystem services (PES) systems?

G iven past trends, what can be expected from a business as usual scenario?

The analysis above shows the conflicting demands for land use, which are unsustainable under business as usual (BAU) scenario. We examine the impact of LUCC change on key earth systems to illustrate what would likely happen under BAU.

Land Use Conversion

LUCC change is posing a grave danger to earth's ecosystems. As discussed above, per capita arable land area is decreasing fast. Rockström et al. (2009) estimate that the safe upper boundary of the global cropland area is 15%, a level that is only about three percentage point of the current cropland of about 12%. However, the UNFCCC Commission on Sustainable Agriculture and Climate Change[11] has concluded that the current global agricultural production has already stepped outside the safe boundary (i.e. maximum amount of food that could be produced under a given climate to provide minimum food requirement of a growing population with minimum impact on the climate) (Beddington et al 2011). In addition to its effect on climate change, the conversion of forest, wetlands and savannas into agricultural land is not sustainable as this reduces the ecosystems capacity to provide regulating services and biodiversity (Elmqvist et al 2011; WBGU 2011; Rockström et al 2009). As will be argued below, sustainable intensification is the only option for achieving food security.

Biodiversity

Recent efforts to increase forest cover through reforestation and afforestation programs have helped to reduce deforestation but they do not fully restore lost biodiversity, which is built over hundreds of years and comprises complex and diverse biomes. Biodiversity trends monitored using the living planet index (LPI) show that since 1970, biodiversity has declined by 30%. The tropics have had a severe decline in biodiversity (about 60%) whereas the temperate regions experienced relative recovery (increase of +15%) (CBD2010). Rockström et al (2009) also report that, on average, more than 100 per million species are lost each year (E/MSY)—a level that is more than 100 times the planetary boundary (10 E/MSY) deemed to be safe operating space for human welfare within the earth system. Current rate of extinction is 100–1000 higher than the Holocene (pre-industrial) age level (0.1 – 1 E/ MSY). BAU is not an option as it has already proven to be unsustainable.

Freshwater Resources

With a rise in population, there is an increase in the quantity of water required for agricultural production, domestic consumption, industrial use and recreation. Currently, about 17% of the 7 billion people experience severe water scarcity (FAO 2011c). Over the past 50 years, freshwater withdrawal tripled (UN-water 2011) while irrigated area increased 117% (FAO 2011a). During the same period, rainfed crop area decreased by 0.2% (FAO 2011). Groundwater is increasingly becoming a major source of irrigation water; by 2009, groundwater accounted for 40% of the volume of irrigation water (Ibid). This is leading to falling water tables and puts at risk the inland arid lands of India, China, the Midwestern United States and the MENA region, which heavily depend on groundwater for irrigation (FAO 2011). Climate change, water pollution and land degradation are all increasing the uncertainties of freshwater resources, further putting pressure on the available freshwater resources. The situation is more alarming in arid areas in developing countries, which experience severe water shortages.

Bioenergy

Demand for energy will increase 35% by 2035 compared to its
2008 level (IAEA 2010). Bioenergy production has been one
solution to addressing this rising demand. Half of the global cereals
consumption in 2005/6–2007/8 was due to US ethanol production
(Hertel 2011) and projections by FAO/OECD (2008) show that
52% of maize and 32% of oilseeds demand to year 2020 will be
due to bioenergy. Estimates show that a large portion of the area
for bioenergy production will be derived from clearing forests
and grassland (Lambin 2010; Hertel 2011). This trend shows the
trade-offs between the global objective of reducing GHG emission
and biodiversity since the conversion of forest and grassland
to bioenergy reduces biodiversity. At the same time, switching
cropland used for food production to bioenergy production will
lead to higher food prices, which in turn will compromise the
global objective of eradicating hunger by 2015. For example, Hertel
et al (2008) estimate that EU and US biofuel mandates will reduce
pastureland in Brazil by about 10% in 2015 from its 2006 level.
How much this reduction in pastureland will affect other land
uses, however, depends on the extent to which stocking densities
of livestock are likely to change (Dumortier et al 2010), which is
often poorly captured by many models of agriculture and land use.
The discussion above suggests the uncertainties of reducing GHG
emission using the BAU (first generation) feedstock. Consideration
for the second generation feedstock have been argued to be a better
option for achieving the environmental objective of reducing GHG.

What Is Achievable?

We explore the prospects for various scenarios and how realistic
the assumptions used in international debates are. We focus our
discussion on food security, climate change and biodiversity. Both
food security and climate change were not a focus of our discussion
on LUCC but they both have been dominating international debate
on sustainable development. The focus on food security is based
on the fact that agriculture contributes the largest share of land

conversion and that recent food price spikes have renewed debates on food security (Fan and Pandya-Lorch 2012). Focus on climate change is largely based on the international debate on mitigation—an aspect which has dominated efforts to increase forest area and forest conservation efforts.

Food Security

The Millennium Development Goals state that by 2015, the share of the people with hunger will be reduced by 50% from its level in 1990 (MDG 2010). This goal has seen limited achievement in developing regions, where the proportion of people suffering from undernourishment was 20% in 1990–92 but fell to only 16% in 2005–07 (MDG 2010). One of the strategies for addressing hunger is to increase agricultural productivity in developing countries. Sustainable agricultural intensification will require adoption of sustainable land and water management practices (FAO 2011a). This includes use of more efficient land management practices and irrigation water (Ibid). Increasing agricultural productivity will be more significant in developing countries where there is still a wide yield gap.

A recent forecasting study showed a decreasing yield growth at global level. The major reason behind the downward trend is the narrowing yield gap in developed countries and major producers in Asia. This means developing regions with wide yield gaps will account for the largest share of production growth to meet the future increase demand. This is achievable but to realize this, constraints which limit higher yield in such regions need to be addressed. These include increased investment in agricultural research as well as addressing market conditions and rural services, which will provide technical support and incentives for increasing productivity. Greater water productivity (Falkenmark and Rockström 2006) is also required to increase yield in the regions where water productivity is low.

A Higher Water Use Efficiency Is Required

The increased demand for water calls for the improvement of water use efficiency to minimize or close the large gap between water supply and demand in the future under land use and water use efficiency (BAU). Under BAU and without use of water for biofuel production, water demand in 2050 will exceed water supply by 3,300 km³. Additional water withdrawal of 5,600 km³/year is required to eliminate hunger and undernourishment and to feed the additional three billion inhabitants in year 2050 (Falkenmark and Rockström 2004). This means almost doubling the current withdrawal of 7,130 km³ 2050 (CA 2007). Decreasing water supply is also a result of many types of land degradation (deforestation and land clearing, crusting, etc). This affects storage and availability of green water (soil moisture), which in turn reduces terrestrial ecosystems capacity to provide biomass and regulating services—such as carbon sequestration (Rockström et al 2009). This means an integrated approach is required to close the gap.

To achieve the required growth crop yield in low income countries and to address the increasing water shortage problem, more efficient water use is required. The average water use efficiency in rainfed systems in the arid and semi-arid areas in Africa is about 5,000 m³ of water per ton of grain, but if supplemental irrigation of only 100 mm per year is used, crop yield doubles and reduces the water use to 2,000 m³ (SIWI et al 2005). At a global scale, improving rainfed water (green water) use efficiency could reduce the water demand by 1,500 km³/year or 80% of the current irrigation water. Expansion and improvement of productivity of the irrigation systems has the capacity to increase 1,800 km³. This would still leave a gap of 3,300 km³ between supply and demand. This means efforts to close the water demand-supply gap should pay due attention to green water—which despite having a large potential to contribute to water demand has received limited attention in water development and management. In addition to food, about 90% of the global green water is required to sustain ecosystems (Rockström 1999).

Biodiversity

The Convention of Biological Diversity (CDB) established a goal to protect at least 10% of ecological regions (CBD 2011). Of the 825 terrestrial ecoregions, regions with large number of species and distinct habitat types, 56% report more than 10% of their protected (CBD 2011). As observed above, the rate of biodiversity loss is almost 10 times the safe earth boundary. Despite the alarming biodiversity loss, the increase in the protected area provides the hope of reducing this unsustainable trend.

Choices for Managing Land Use for Multiple Objectives and Critical Areas of Global Coordination

Since land area is fixed, all types of land uses are competing for the same land. The choices have to be defined by the ultimate benefits of land use—human welfare. As argued throughout this paper, all ecosystem components have an intricate interrelationship with one another. For brevity, our discussion below focuses on a selected number of choices with significant and direct trade-offs only.

For example, the mitigation of climate change under UNFCCC, conservation of biodiversity under CBD and prevention of land degradation under UNCCD by their nature are interdependent and could be simultaneously achieved. A recent international workshop promoted a nexus approach in which programs on interdependent ecosystems—such as food security, water and energy—are planned and implemented in a synergistic way. An example of synergistic objective is the Niger's reforestation program—which has covered 5 million hectares of planted or protected trees—provides 0.5 million tons of grain per year and sequesters carbon (Beddington et al 2011). The trees also provided fuelwood, medicinal plants and improved soil fertility. The world is increasingly realizing this potential and international cooperation on environmental management and governance has increased in the past two decades (Biermann et al 2010).

Regarding food, bioenergy, biodiversity, and reduction of GHG emissions, the world has to balance the three objectives using integrated LUCC modeling to find solutions which maximize human welfare. Studies have cast doubt on the efficacy of biofuels as mechanisms for reducing GHG using current technologies. In an attempt to achieve this, the current EU biofuel sustainability criteria passed in 2009, requires that liquid bioenergy should lead to CHG emission reduction of at least 35% and gradually increasing to 60% and should not be produced from raw materials grown on land of high biodiversity value or carbon stock (Nillson and Persson 2012). Such mandate considers two objectives—GHG emission reduction and conservation of biodiversity and sets an example of multiple objectives mandates. However, the EU biofuel sustainability mandate does not directly address food security aspects and does not consider indirect LUCC (iLUCC) (CEC, 2010). Achieving the EU biofuel sustainability mandate is a challenge since it does not consider iLUCC and it requires a constantly updated biodiversity data in order to trace the impact of feedstock production on biodiversity. This could be a big challenge in developing countries—especially in countries with weak institutions.[12]

Second generation feedstock is being advocated to reduce the food-bioenergy trade-offs. Research is needed to develop the second generation feedstock and renewable energy with minimal or no competition with food production. For example Gates (2011) notes that US investment in renewable energy is low and increasing research investment will have long term payoffs.

The agriculture sector is often not given the political attention and commitment that it deserves, especially in developing countries where trends over the last two decades indicate reduced allocation of national development budgets to agriculture. Furthermore there has also been a substantial decline in multilateral lending and bilateral aid for this sector. This trend is contrary to the increasing global cooperation on environmental conservation. The two food price spikes in the past five years should be seen as a wake-up call for national governments and the international community to invest in agriculture. This will help close the wide potential-actual yield gap in developing regions and consequently reduce land conversion to agriculture. However, agriculture investments should be made with multiple choices—ensuring food security and environmental objectives are addressed.

Achieving food security also requires reducing post-harvest losses, which are high in both developing and developed countries. Post-harvest food losses could be reduced by investment in processing and storage investment in developing countries and by public awareness in developed countries. Reduction in post-harvest losses will enhance food security and reduce the demand for additional land, energy and other resources.

Prospects for International Instruments for Land Use Change Management

International market conditions provide a great potential for ensuring sustainable land and water management practices for ecosystems. Recent development in the carbon market illustrates the increasing international cooperation. Until the mid-1990s, international carbon market was negligible (Mol 2012). However, the climate change mitigation efforts broke what Beck (2005) called the national-state container and international carbon markets have increased dramatically (Mol 2012). The success stories in Brazil, Indonesia discussed earlier demonstrate progress, which could be made if international support is given to a country with strong policies and strategies to address unsustainable land conversions. Daunting challenges remain on implementing various global environmental programs. But the increasing international cooperation in land and water management has increased significantly since the first Rio summit in 1992—thanks to United Nations concerted efforts to promote international cooperation (Sanwal 2004). Participation of the private companies and voluntary carbon market (VCM) initiatives by environmentally conscious companies also offers some opportunities for improving carbon markets but as discussed below, market based strategies still face challenges in countries with poorly developed markets and institutions. Though VCM only accounted for 0.3% of carbon traded in 2010 (World Bank 2011a), it is increasing and offers an opportunity to expand if conducive environment is created to enhance participation.

However, implementation of PES [payments for ecosystem services] has been expensive and in some cases hard due to the weak institutions in developing countries—where it is cheaper to pay for PES and where degradation of biodiversity is more severe. For example, Bruce et al (2010) observed weak land tenure systems in areas high carbon density. The fragile states could also fail to meet the REDD+ and other international requirements, hence limiting their applicability and effectiveness. This means implementing PES may need to incorporate capacity building of local and national governance structure in fragile states.

The prospects of climate change negotiations are not bright and the carbon market trend levelled off in 2009 and showed a slight decline in 2010. This puts into jeopardy the international cooperation on climate change and on other initiatives. Of concern are the uncertainties surrounding the compliance market and additionality. For example, most decisions and rules and regulations on the REDD+ funded by governments and international organizations are still pending.

As argued above, synergistic programs—providing several ecosystem services are more likely to have greater pay-off and be more sustainable than single-objective programs. This suggests the international cooperation on carbon and other ecosystem service initiatives need to explore synergies among national and international sustainable development conventions such as UNCCD, CBD, UNFCCC and others should explore closer collaboration to achieve synergistic their objectives, namely, combating land degradation, conservation of biodiversity and carbon sequestration. This is in line with the Agenda 21 spirit which promoted cooperation and building on synergies among ecosystem initiatives. A new approach is also called for to strengthen the economic incentives for sustainable land use on a strong evidence base. Such an approach following a cost of action versus cost of inaction approach regarding land and soil degradation could go a long way toward mobilizing public and private investment for sustainable land use. A related initiative on "Economics of land degradation" (ELD) has been started in 2011 by UNCCD, Germany and the European Commission (Nkonya et al. 2011).

Notes

1. We follow the FAO definition of forest—a land mass with at least 10% of its area covered by trees.

2. The goals are: 1. Promote the conservation of the biological diversity of ecosystems, habitats and biomes; 2. Promote the conservation of species diversity; 3. Promote the conservation of genetic diversity; 4. Promote sustainable use and consumption; 5. Pressures from habitat loss, land use change and degradation, and unsustainable water use, reduced; 6. Control threats from invasive alien species; 7. Address challenges to biodiversity from climate change, and pollution; 8. Maintain capacity of ecosystems to deliver goods and services and support livelihoods; 9. Maintain sociocultural diversity of indigenous and local communities; 10. Ensure the fair and equitable sharing of benefits arising out of the use of genetic resources; 11. Parties have improved financial, human, scientific, technical & technological capacity to implement the Convention.

3. Brazil and the Congo are respectively the first and second countries with largest tropical forest area.

4. After Nigeria and Ethiopia, with populations of 160 million and 84 million people respectively (FAOSTAT 2011).

5. See ClientEarth (2009) for an analysis of WTO jurisprudence about trade of natural resources.

6. www.theredddesk.org/activity/memorandum_of_understanding_on_environmental _cooperation_between_the_state_of_acre_of_the_f

7. http://news.mongabay.com/2009/0915-cerrado.html

8. LUCC was an International geosphere-biosphere program (IGBP) and international human dimensions of global environmental change program (IHDP) project, which organized a workshop to discuss land use and land cover change (Veldkamp and Lambin 2001).

9. Ehlirch and Ehlrich (2009) revisited the "population bomb" publication and argued that its main message is still valid, though they admit the exaggeration resulting from the sensationalist title.

10. Following Brazil's commitment at the climate change summit in 2008 to reduce deforestation in the Amazon to 20% of its rate in 1996–2005, Norway committed US$1 billion to support achievement of this target. The Brazilian government also initiated a

forest moratorium, by paying ranchers and soy bean farmers who do not cut the forest. The protected area of the Amazon was also increased (Nepstadt et al 2010).

11. Formed in 2011 as part of the UNFCCC COP-17 to synthesize empirical evidence into policy actions for achieving global food security given the climate change (Beddington et al 2011).

12. See further discussion on international instruments below.

13. Land rent theory assumes that a land parcel is allocated such that it earns the highest possible rent given its attributes and location.

> *"The adoption of specific policies can influence land-use changes and increase the expected provision of some ecosystem services but at the expense of others; there seem to be inevitable tradeoffs among services."*

There Is Not an Infinite Supply of Land to Convert for a Growing Population

Leighton Walker Kille

In the following viewpoint, Leighton Walker Kille argues that, with projected increases in population in the coming century, biodiversity will suffer. And that, in turn, will hurt humanity. The author cites a study that uses modeling to predict how the next thirty-five years will play out under five different scenarios. As with many of the viewpoints in this resource, the researchers conclude that the adoption of certain specific policies can influence changes in land use. However, they caution, these can come at the expense of other ecosystem services. Kille is a research editor for Journalist's Resource.

"The impact of Future U.S. Land-Use Change on Urban Areas, Forests, Habitat and Biodiversity," by Leighton Walker Kille, Journalist's Resource, May 29, 2014. https://journalistsresource.org/studies/environment/ecology/future-land-use-change-urban-areas-forests-habitat-biodiversity. Licensed under CC BY-ND 4.0.

As you read, consider the following questions:

1. According to the viewpoint, what is the projected world population for 2050?
2. What species modeled in the study are most sensitive to land-use change?
3. What was the only policy that significantly influenced how metropolitan areas grew?

According to the Census Bureau, the population of the United States will exceed 416 million by 2060, up from 309 million in 2010, the year of the last full census. Coincidentally, the increase is nearly the same as the entire US population in 1910, 92 million. All those millions of people will need places to live and food to eat, naturally, and the question becomes where and how—and what the environmental consequences of our choices will be.

Research has shown that humans are having a growing impact on the planet's ecosystem, taking a larger share of the biosphere's production. Research from Yale, Texas A&M and Boston University published in 2012 found that worldwide, nearly 6 million square kilometers of land could be urbanized by 2030. And as low-density sprawl pushes outward in both the developed and developing world, so too do cultivated lands: A 2012 study in *Proceedings of the National Academy of Sciences* found that we will have to nearly double the land under cultivation to feed the world's projected population of more than 9 billion people in 2050.

However, there is not an infinite supply of land to convert to farms, suburbs, malls and highways. Moreover, with every acre that's covered in asphalt or plowed under, biodiversity suffers, and that's not something we can do without: A 2012 metastudy published in the journal *Nature* reviewed more than 20 years of research on biodiversity and found "unequivocal evidence" that its loss reduces the efficiency with which ecosystems capture resources, produce biomass and decompose and recycle biologically essential nutrients—ones that, in turn, feed humanity.

CLIMATE IMPACTS OF LAND USE ARE UNDERESTIMATED

When it comes to tackling climate change, the focus often falls on reducing the use of fossil fuels and developing sustainable energy sources. But a new Cornell-led study shows that deforestation and subsequent use of lands for agriculture or pasture, especially in tropical regions, contribute more to climate change than previously thought.

The new paper, "Are the Impacts of Land Use on Warming Underestimated in Climate Policy?" published Aug. 2 in *Environmental Research Letters*, also shows just how significantly that impact has been underestimated. Even if all fossil fuel emissions are eliminated, if current tropical deforestation rates hold steady through 2100, there will still be a 1.5 degree increase in global warming.

"A lot of the emphasis of climate policy is on converting to sustainable energy from fossil fuels," said Natalie M. Mahowald, the paper's lead author and a professor in the Department of Earth and Atmospheric Sciences and faculty director of environment for the Atkinson Center for a Sustainable Future. "It's an incredibly important step to take, but, ironically, particulates released from the burning of fossil fuels—which are severely detrimental to human health— have a cooling effect on the climate. Removing those particulates actually makes it harder to reach the lower temperatures laid out in the Paris agreement."

A 2014 study in *Proceedings of the National Academy of Sciences,* "Projected Land-use Change Impacts on Ecosystem Services in the United States," looks at how the next 35 years could play out. Using an econometric model, the authors project land-use change in the contiguous United States from 2001 to 2051 under five scenarios: (1) Continuation of land-use trends experienced from 1992 to 1997, called the "1990s trend." (2) High commodity prices that create pressures to convert more land to agricultural use, similar to the period from 2007 to 2012; this is referred to as the "high crop demand" model. (3) $100-per-acre incentives to

She said that in addition to phasing out fossil fuels, scientific and policymaking communities must pay attention to changes in land use to stem global warming, as deforestation effects are "not negligible."

While the carbon dioxide collected by trees and plants is released during the cutting and burning of deforestation, other greenhouse gases—specifically nitrous oxide and methane—are released after natural lands have been converted to agricultural and other human usage. The gases compound the effect of the carbon dioxide's ability to trap the sun's energy within the atmosphere, contributing to radiative forcing—energy absorbed by the Earth versus energy radiated off—and a warmer climate.

As a result, while only 20 percent of the rise in carbon dioxide caused by human activity originates from land use and land-cover change, that warming proportion from land use (compared with other human activities) increases to 40 percent once co-emissions like nitrous oxide and methane are factored in.

"In the short term, the land use tends to have twice the radiative forcing as it should have had from the carbon dioxide because of the co-emissions, so it's twice as important," said Mahowald.

"Research: Climate Impacts of Land Use Are Underestimated," by David Nutt, Cornell.edu, August 30, 2017.

increase forestation and reduce deforestation. (4) $100-per-acre incentives to conserve natural habitats, including forests, grasslands and shrub lands. (5) Restrictions on the expansion of urban and suburban sprawl, with the goal of concentrating growth in existing metropolitan areas. Changes were calculated only for privately owned land; public lands were assumed to remain unchanged.

With the five scenarios, the goal was to see how market forces, channeled by each incentive, would shape long-term changes in land use and subsequently ecosystem services, wildlife habitat and biodiversity. Some of the financial incentives were structured as taxes, others as subsidies to see what the effects would be. The study's findings include:

- The two baseline scenarios—the 1990s trend and high crop demand—both resulted in rapid expansion of urbanized areas and loss of rangelands and pasture. Loss of cropland under the 1990s trend was 11.2 million hectares (27.7 million acres); under the high crop demand scenario losses rose to 28.2 million hectares (69.7 million acres). Forest land increased modestly under both scenarios, but with patterns of gains and losses.

- Urban land is projected to increase by 26.2 million hectares (64.7 million acres) under the 1990s trend and 29.5 million hectares (72.9 million acres) with high crop demand. These represent, respectively, a 63% and 71% increase from 2001 to 2051.

- Food production increased significantly under both scenarios, with the number of kilocalories produced rising 50% under the 1990s trend and doubling with high crop demand. "Increases in food production are driven by increases in crop yield (which we assume will increase by 6% every five years) and changes in agriculture area." The researchers cautioned that the gains could be overoptimistic if the growth in yields is linear rather than exponential.

- Under the baseline scenarios, the habitat of 25% of the species modeled declined by 10% or more: "The four groups of species (amphibians, influential species, game species, and at-risk birds) responded in broadly similar ways to the two future scenarios. At-risk birds are the most sensitive to land-use change. Roughly one-third of these species are projected to lose more than 10% of their habitat."

- The $100-per-acre forest incentive resulted in the addition of 30.6 million hectares (75.6 million acres) of forest land, a rise of 14% over the baseline. The increase was primarily the result of rangeland, cropland and pasture being converted to forest.

- Biomass grew significantly with forest incentives, increasing 8% relative to baseline, while timber production rose 18%. Food production decreased by 10% compared with the 1990s trend baseline scenario.
- The $100-per-acre habitat conservation incentive increased rangeland by 12.4 million hectares (30.6 million acres), a rise of 5% relative to the baseline. Most of the increase comes at the expense of crops and pasture, with little change in forests. Carbon storage, timber production and food production all dropped slightly.
- The habitats conservation policy had the strongest positive effect on habitat of all the scenarios: 31% of species gained 10% or more in habitat area by 2051. For the forest incentive, only 13% of species had the same habitat gain, and 16% for the urban containment policy. "Both forest incentives and urban containment policies also result in more species gaining than losing at least 10% in habitat area."
- Urban containment was the only policy that significantly influenced how metropolitan areas grew. It held urban growth to 12.2 million hectares (30.1 million acres), compared to a baseline increase of 29.5 million hectares (72.9 million acres) under the high crop demand scenario—59% less. Urban containment also resulted in slight increases in forest, rangeland and pastures.
- The costs of the incentives for forests and habitat varied significantly: The forest incentive required approximately $7.5 billion in annual government subsidies to landowners, a consequence of the ease with which agricultural land can be converted to forest. In contrast, the natural habitats incentive policy generated a positive cash flow for the government of approximately $1.8 billion annually.

"Our results show that differences in the underlying drivers of land-use change, such as changes in future crop prices, can have large impacts on projected land-use change with cascading effects on the provision of ecosystem services," the researchers conclude.

"The adoption of specific policies can influence land-use changes and increase the expected provision of some ecosystem services but at the expense of others; there seem to be inevitable tradeoffs among services."

Related Research

A 2013 study in *Proceedings of the National Academy of Sciences* (*PNAS*), "Global Human Appropriation of Net Primary Production Doubled in the 20th Century," analyzes humankind's growing impact on the biosphere, from our consumption of food, organic materials and other products of sun-powered energy, to our effect on the composition of the atmosphere, biodiversity and food webs. It found that from 1910 to 2005, human population grew nearly fourfold—from 1.7 billion to 6.5 billion people—while economic output increased 17-fold. Over the same time, human appropriation of net primary biosphere production doubled. While proportionally lower growth in biosphere appropriation is a positive, it still increased from 13% in 1910 to 25% in 2005, meaning that humans currently appropriate a full quarter of the net primary productivity of the biosphere.

> *"The main motivations for adopting the technologies or practices were found to be potential production increases (24%), profit increases (20%), improvement of well-being and livelihood (20%) and reduced workload (5%)."*

Land Users Are Positive About Long-Term Benefits of Sustainable Practices

Markus Giger

In the following viewpoint, Markus Giger argues that analysis of data from a global archive finds that land users perceive sustainable land management practices in a positive light for the short term—less than three years—and a very positive light for the long term—ten years or more. The study's authors recommend engaging in sustainable agriculture practices, such as structural measures, agronomic measures, vegetative measures, and management measures. Giger is head of sustainability for the Centre for Development and Environment at the University of Bern.

As you read, consider the following questions:

1. How many case studies did the study's authors analyze?
2. What percentage of participants had a positive or very positive view of the long term?
3. According to the author, what factor of the data analysis could skew cost-benefit perceptions?

The costs and benefits of sustainable land management have been collated in a new review. Data from a global archive was analysed for the costs of sustainable practices and technologies and for land users' perceptions of cost-benefit ratios. Most respondents had a positive view of the short-term cost-benefit ratio, and a strongly positive view of the long term. Low upfront costs, long-term planning and security of land tenure were identified as important factors to facilitate these practices.

Economic factors are key to the adoption of sustainable farming practices. Upfront costs can be barriers even if there are accepted long-term economic benefits. There is a pressing global need for the adoption of improved techniques, as land degradation—which includes effects such as losses in soil fertility, soil erosion, and lowering of the water table—leads to losses in productivity and disruption to ecosystem services.

Sustainable land management refers to a wide range of practices and technologies that prevent, mitigate or rehabilitate damage to land, therefore protecting or enhancing the natural resources of that land and its surroundings. There are structural measures, such as terraces, banks and dams; agronomic measures, such as mulching and increasing organic matter in soil; vegetative measures, such as tree planting and hedging; and management measures, such as grazing timing and change of species compositions.

The authors assessed data from 363 case studies conducted internationally between 1990 and 2012 which are held by the World Overview of Conservation Approaches and Technologies (WOCAT). 46% of studies were from Africa, 41% from Asia,

7% from Europe, and a small portion from South America and Australia.

Costs were separated into those relating to establishment and maintenance, and adjusted for inflation and currency conversion to constant 2010 US dollars. "Short-term" was defined as three years or less, and "long-term" as 10 years or more.

The authors identified data on 258 different sustainable land management technologies. They had median establishment costs of 500 US$/hectare. Values ranged from less than 20 to over 5000, with half of all cases between 193 and 1918 US$/ha. The median annual maintenance costs were 100 US$/ha, with half of all cases between 27 and 324 US$/ha.

The results show a large discrepancy in establishment and maintenance costs, due to the wide range of sustainable land management interventions. Technologies which involve significant infrastructure, such as the management of water flows or afforestation, are high-cost, whereas certain management adjustments, such as land-use change or changes in timing of activities, would incur very few costs.

In terms of perceptions of the cost-benefit ratio of sustainable land management, 73% of case study participants had a positive or neutral perception in the short term, whilst 97% had a positive or very positive view of the long term.

The main motivations for adopting the technologies or practices were found to be potential production increases (24%), profit increases (20%), improvement of well-being and livelihood (20%) and reduced workload (5%).

One limitation to the study is that land users in the WOCAT database are not likely to represent typical land users. Many of the case studies in the database are already involved in sustainable land management projects—particularly projects recognised as "promising or good"—so may have an above-average chance of having a positive cost-benefit ratio.

Furthermore, 57% of the cases studied received financial support from development projects or government programmes, which could skew cost-benefit perceptions. Nevertheless, the authors emphasise the finding that in the remaining cases (43%), the establishment costs were fully covered by land users.

The recommendations from the authors are relevant for encouraging more sustainable agriculture; short-term support can help overcome the barriers of sustainable land management set-up costs, and secure tenure rights can help land-users plan for the long- term, resulting in benefits for producers, consumers and the environment.

Periodical and Internet Sources Bibliography

The following articles have been selected to supplement the diverse views presented in this chapter.

Emily Badget, "The Bipartisan Cry of 'Not in My Backyard,'"
New York Times, August 21, 2018. https://www.nytimes
.com/2018/08/21/upshot/home-ownership-nimby-bipartisan
.html.

Dan Charles, "For One City Manager, Climate Becomes a Matter of
Conscience," NPR, December 19, 2018. https://www.npr
.org/2018/12/19/677769617/for-one-city-manager-climate
-becomes-a-matter-of-conscience.

Daniel DiMartino, "Unleash the Potential of Federal Lands,"
Foundation for Economic Education, July 14, 2018. https://
fee.org/articles/unleash-the-potential-of-federal-lands.

Economist, "The EPA Is Rewriting the Most Important Number
in Climate Economics," November 16, 2017. https://www
.economist.com/united-states/2017/11/16/the-epa-is-rewriting
-the-most-important-number-in-climate-economics?zid
=313&ah=fe2aac0b11adef572d67aed9273b6e55.

Emily Guerin, "California Housing Development Is a 'Disaster
Waiting to Happen,'" NPR, January 1, 2019. https://www.npr
.org/2019/01/01/681368083/california-housing-development
-is-a-disaster-waiting-to-happen.

Matthew Mason, "What Is Sustainability and Why Is It Important?,"
EnvironmentalScience.org. https://www.environmentalscience
.org/sustainability.

Fred Smith and Iain Murray, "The State Can't Protect the
Environment—Markets Can," Foundation for Economic
Education, March 18, 2017. https://fee.org/articles/the-state
-cant-protect-the-environment-markets-can.

Paul West, "Mind the Gaps: Reducing Hunger by Improving Yields
on Small Farms," Conversation, January 23, 2017. https://
theconversation.com/mind-the-gaps-reducing-hunger-by
-improving-yields-on-small-farms-67287.

For Further Discussion

Chapter 1

1. How can land use change both benefit a society and come at a price?
2. How does the development of land for agriculture impact the environment differently than urban areas?
3. How do rising populations in the world's cities present challenges to the environment?

Chapter 2

1. Should developers be reined in by stricter regulation?
2. What methods can be implemented to make agriculture more sustainable?
3. Does the data from various studies on the topic seem to agree, more or less, or are findings contradictory?

Chapter 3

1. Which should take priority: the mining of natural resources to help a country's economy or long-term considerations for the environment? Why?
2. Why have humans been blamed for deforestation and other acts that have caused destruction to earth?
3. Is responsible development worth it if it is only undertaken by some countries and not all?

Chapter 4

1. What are some considerations to take when planning an urban neighborhood?
2. Are some improvements better than none when it comes to the environment?
3. What has the better chance of changing practices of land-use change and development: government policies or individual efforts? Why?

Organizations to Contact

The editors have compiled the following list of organizations concerned with the issues debated in this book. The descriptions are derived from materials provided by the organizations. All have publications or information available for interested readers. The list was compiled on the date of publication of the present volume; the information provided here may change. Be aware that many organizations take several weeks or longer to respond to inquiries, so allow as much time as possible.

Bureau of Land Management

1849 C Street NW, Room 5665
Washington, DC 20240
(202) 208-3801
email: blm_press@blm.gov
website: https://www.blm.gov

The Bureau of Land Management works to sustain the health, diversity, and productivity of public lands for the use and enjoyment of present and future generations. The bureau manages public lands for a variety of uses, such as energy development, livestock grazing, recreation, and timber harvesting. At the same time, the organization works to ensure that natural, cultural, and historical resources are maintained.

Environmental Literacy Council

1625 K Street NW, Suite 1020
Washington, DC 20006
(202) 296-0390
website: https://www.enviroliteracy.org

The Environmental Literacy Council is an independent nonprofit made up of scientists, economists, and educators striving to connect teachers and students to science-based information on environmental issues. The organization's website offers over one thousand pages of background information and resources on environmental topics, along with curricular materials and textbook reviews.

Food and Water Watch

1616 P Street NW
Washington, DC 20036
(202) 683-2500
email: info@fwwatch.org
website: https://www.foodandwaterwatch.org

Food and Water Watch works to achieve healthy food and clean water for everyone on the planet. The organization advocates for individuals over corporations and for a democracy that improves human lives and the environment.

National Parks and Conservation Association

777 Sixth Street NW, Suite 700
Washington, DC 20001-3723
(800) 628-7275
email: npca@npca.org
website: https://www.npca.org

The National Parks and Conservation Association champions America's national parks, working with program and policy experts, volunteers, lobbyists, community organizers, and communications specialists to protect and preserve the country's national parks.

National Park Service

1849 C Street NW
Washington, DC 20240
(202) 208-6843
email: www.nps.gov/aboutus/contact-form.htm?o= 4A96D0B58DC08FB284A85DA8F601&r=/aboutus /contactus.htm
website: https://www.nps.gov

The National Park Service preserves the natural and cultural resources and values of the National Park System. The twenty thousand employees help local governments, nonprofits, businesses, tribes, and individuals revitalize their communities, preserve local history, and celebrate local heritage.

Project Drawdown

27 Gate 5 Road
Sausalito, CA 94965
email: info@drawdown.org
website: https://www.drawdown.org

Project Drawdown gathers and facilitates a broad coalition of researchers, scientists, graduate students, PhDs, postdocs, policy makers, business leaders, and activists to assemble and present the best available information on climate solutions in order to describe their beneficial financial, social, and environmental impact over the next thirty years.

Property and Environment Research Center

2048 Analysis Drive, Suite A
Bozeman MT 59718
(406) 587-9591
email: perc@perc.org
website: https://www.perc.org

The Property and Environment Research Center is a conservation and research institute dedicated to free market environmentalism. The center promotes creative conservation and environmental entrepreneurship. The organization works with a variety of sectors to understand the root of environmental conflict and identify solutions.

Public Lands Alliance

2401 Blueridge Avenue, Suite 303
Silver Spring, MD 20902
(301) 946-9475
email: http://www.publiclandsalliance.org/contactus
website: http://www.publiclandsalliance.org

Public Lands Alliance is devoted to building effective nonprofit organizations and public-nonprofit partnerships with the goal of preserving public lands as well as raising awareness of conservation and preservation efforts. The alliance maintains an extensive and vibrant network of community members, agency leaders, socially conscious corporations, elected officials, and policy makers.

US Department of Agriculture (USDA)

1400 Independence Avenue SW
Washington, DC 20250
(202) 720-2791
website: https://www.usda.gov

The USDA is a government agency that provides leadership on food, agriculture, natural resources, rural development, and nutrition in the United States based on public policy and scientific research.

US Environmental Protection Agency (EPA)

1200 Pennsylvania Avenue NW
Washington, DC 20460
(202) 564-4700
website: https://www.epa.gov

The EPA is a government organization whose mission is to protect the health of humans and the environment. To achieve is mission, the EPA gives grants; studies environmental issues; partners with businesses, nonprofit organizations, and state and local governments; and educates the public about the environment.

US Forest Service

1400 Independence Avenue SW
Washington, DC 20250-1111
(800) 832-1355
website: https://www.fs.fed.us

The US Forest Service is a part of the US Department of Agriculture. The agency's mission is to sustain the health, diversity, and productivity of the nation's forests and grasslands to meet the needs of present and future generations. It manages and protects 154 national forests and 20 grasslands.

Urban Land Institute

2001 L Street NW, Suite 200
Washington, DC 20036-4948
(202) 624-7000
email: customerservice@uli.org
website: https://americas.uli.org

The Urban Land Institute provides leadership in the responsible use of land and in creating and sustaining thriving communities worldwide. With forty thousand members worldwide, the institute sets standards of excellence in development practice.

Bibliography of Books

Robert Albritton, *Let Them Eat Junk*. London, England: Pluto Press, 2009.

Stephanie Anderson, *One Size Fits None: A Farm Girl's Search for the Promise of Regenerative Agriculture*. Lincoln: University of Nebraska Press, 2019.

Jonathan Barnett and Brian William Blaessser, *Reinventing Development Regulations*. Cambridge, MA: Lincoln Institute of Land Policy, 2017.

Robin Lee Chazdon, *Second Growth: The Promise of Tropical Forest Regeneration in an Age of Deforestation*. Chicago, IL: University of Chicago Press, 2014.

Sarah Williams Goldhagen, *Welcome to Your World: How the Built Environment Shapes Our Lives*. New York, NY: HarperCollins Publishers, 2017.

Toby Hemenway, *The Permaculture City: Regenerative Design for Urban, Suburban, and Town Resilience*. White River Junction, VT: Chelsea Green Publishing, 2014.

Martin Mowforth, *The Violence of Development*. London, England: Pluto Press, 2014.

Jono Neiger, *The Permaculture Promise: What Permaculture Is and How It Can Help Us Reverse Climate Change, Build a More Resilient Future on Earth, Revitalize Our Communities*. North Adams, MA: Storey Publishing, 2016.

John Nolon, *Protecting the Local Environment Through Land Use Law: Standing Ground*. Washington, DC: Environmental Law Institute, 2014.

T. R. Oke, *Urban Climates*. Cambridge, England: Cambridge University Press, 2017.

Christina D. Rosan and Hamil Pearsall, *Growing a Sustainable City? The Question of Urban Agriculture.* Toronto, ON, Canada: University of Toronto Press, 2018.

Christiane Runyan and Paolo D'Odorico, *Global Deforestation.* New York, NY: Cambridge University Press, 2016.

Mark Shepard and Anna Lappe, *Restoration Agriculture: Real-World Permaculture for Farmers.* Austin, TX: Acres USA, 2014.

Josh Tickell, *Kiss the Ground: How the Food You Eat Can Reverse Climate Change, Heal Your Body and Ultimately Save Our World.* New York, NY: Simon & Schuster, 2018.

Eric Toensmeier, *Carbon Farming Solution: A Global Toolkit of Perennial Crops and Regenerative Agriculture Practices.* White River Junction, VT: Chelsea Green Publishing, 2016.

Index

V

W